Unveiling Big Data's Secrets

Data Science for the Big Data Era: Harnessing Insights for Success

Ethan Black

Table of Contents

INTRODUCTION

Data has become essential to organizations in the rapidly changing digital landscape, influencing how we develop, make decisions, and compete in a world where connections are becoming increasingly interconnected. Massive amounts of data are being produced at a never-before-seen rate in the Big Data age. It is now critical to gather, examine, and draw conclusions from this enormous body of data as the amount of data keeps growing. Welcome to the field of data science, where the goal of gaining knowledge from data is achieved by combining art and science.

"Unveiling Big Data's Secrets: Data Science for the Big Data Era - Harnessing Insights for Success" is your essential guide to navigating the fascinating and transformative landscape of data science in the era of Big Data. From the foundations of Big Data to the complexities of data science methodology, tools, and best practices, we set out on a journey that unfolds in these pages. This book will provide the skills and information required to thrive in the data-driven world, regardless of your experience level. You may be an aspiring data scientist, an experienced data professional, or a company executive looking to use data for competitive advantage.

We start by dissecting the notion of big data, investigating the five key elements that define it—volume, velocity, variety, veracity, and value—and investigating the extraordinary expansion that has led to this data revolution. Through case studies and real-world instances, you will understand the scope and importance of our current data challenges.

To get started on the data science path, it is essential to lay a strong foundation. We demystify data science in this book by outlining its definition, methodology, and importance. We'll look at the lifetime of data science and the vital role data scientists play. We'll outline the essential abilities and resources needed to succeed in this industry.

Data is the foundation of data science and frequently comes unorganized. The specifics of collecting and preparing data are covered in detail in Chapter 3. You'll discover how to collect data, clean and preprocess it, and deal with missing data—all crucial aspects of the data science process.

EDA, or exploratory data analysis, is a skill that data scientists practice before tackling more complicated models and algorithms. This vital stage is covered in detail in Chapter 4, where we also discuss data visualization, descriptive statistics, and the art of finding patterns and abnormalities in your data that you may have been unaware of.

The center of data science is machine learning, examined in the context of big data in Chapter 5. Our courses will provide you with the necessary knowledge to make wise judgments in machine learning, covering everything from supervised and unsupervised learning to deep learning and algorithm selection.

Data science is propelled by big data technology. We explore distributed computing, data processing, and storage in Chapter 6, emphasizing important technologies like Spark and Hadoop that help us efficiently address Big Data concerns.

Large data entails large responsibility. Data governance, privacy, security, and ethical issues are covered in detail in Chapter 7. We'll talk about adhering to data regulations and the significance of developing a framework for ethical data science.

Creating actionable insights from data is the focus of Chapter 8. You'll learn about data visualization, prescriptive and predictive analytics, and practical case studies highlighting the effectiveness of making decisions based on data.

Successfully completing a data science project takes more than just technical expertise. The practical components of managing projects, assembling a data science team, and measuring performance are covered in Chapter 9, which will help you ensure your data initiatives are helpful in the real world.

Chapter 10 finally looks into the crystal ball to investigate new developments in data science, AI, and responsible data usage. We'll discuss the future for data-driven enterprises as technology develops further.

Remember that this book is your gateway to understanding the art and science of data in the Big Data era, so keep that in mind as we set out on this adventure through the data science landscape. Every chapter aims to provide you with helpful knowledge and abilities you can use immediately in your career.

Let's go on this adventure together, regardless of your goals—making data-driven decisions, starting a career in data science, or steering your company toward the future of data-driven innovation. Get ready to explore the vast realm of data science and big data, where the opportunities are as endless as the data itself.

CHAPTER I

Understanding Big Data

What is Big Data?

In today's digitally interconnected world, data is being generated unprecedentedly. It flows from every corner of our lives, from social media interactions and online purchases to sensor readings in smart cities and the vast archives of scientific research. This exponential growth in data has given rise to a phenomenon known as Big Data, a term that has become ubiquitous in discussions surrounding technology, business, and society. But what exactly is Big Data, and why is it so significant?

At its core, Big Data is the massive volumes of structured as well as unstructured data that inundate us daily. These datasets are characterized by the "3Vs": volume, velocity, and variety.

Firstly, volume refers to the sheer quantity of data. Unlike traditional datasets that can be easily managed and analyzed with conventional tools, Big Data is massive, often exceeding terabytes, petabytes, or even exabytes in size. This staggering volume necessitates specialized infrastructure and techniques for storage and processing.

Secondly, velocity denotes the speed at which data is generated and must be processed. In the digital age, data streams in real-time, thanks to the proliferation of sensors, devices, and online activities. This rapid influx requires systems capable of processing data swiftly, making decisions in the blink of an eye, and supporting applications that demand near-instantaneous responses.

Finally, variety highlights the diverse nature of Big Data. It encompasses structured data, such as databases and spreadsheets, and unstructured or semi-structured data, including text, images, videos, and social media posts. The variety of data sources and formats presents a challenge: integrating, analyzing, and extracting insights from this heterogeneous landscape.

However, the concept of Big Data extends beyond the 3Vs. It incorporates two additional dimensions: veracity and value. Veracity pertains to the reliability and trustworthiness of the data. With the vast amount of data being generated, its accuracy, completeness, and consistency are often uncertain. Addressing these concerns is essential to ensure that decisions based on Big Data are sound and reliable.

Perhaps the most crucial aspect of Big Data is its potential to unlock value. The value dimension encapsulates the idea that, when harnessed effectively, Big Data can yield insights, drive innovation, and create tangible benefits. These benefits span a broad spectrum, from enhancing business operations and optimizing supply chains to improving healthcare outcomes and supporting scientific research.

Organizations have turned to advanced technologies and methodologies to harness the potential of Big Data. Among these is distributed computing, which involves using clusters of interconnected computers to process and store data. Technologies like Hadoop and Spark have emerged as critical tools for handling Big Data workloads, enabling parallel processing and fault tolerance at scale.

Machine learning and artificial intelligence (AI) are integral in extracting insights from Big Data. These technologies can uncover patterns, correlations, and predictive models within massive datasets, offering valuable intelligence for businesses, governments, and researchers alike.

Moreover, data visualization has become indispensable in making Big Data understandable and actionable. By creating intuitive visual representations of complex datasets, data visualization tools empower decision-makers to grasp trends, identify outliers, and communicate findings effectively.

The rise of Big Data has also led to an increased focus on data privacy, security, and ethics. As organizations collect and analyze vast amounts of personal information, questions about consent, data ownership, and responsible data usage have become paramount. Regulations such as the General Data Protection Regulation and California Consumer Privacy Act are just some legal frameworks addressing these concerns.

In conclusion, Big Data is not merely about the quantity of data but encompasses its velocity, variety, veracity, and most importantly, its potential value. In our data-driven age, harnessing and making sense of Big Data is a strategic advantage for businesses, a catalyst for scientific discoveries, and a driver of innovation across sectors. It is a transformative force that continues to shape our digital landscape, offering opportunities and challenges that will define our future. Understanding what Big Data is and how to leverage it effectively is essential for individuals, organizations, and societies looking to thrive in our data-rich world.

Big Data Characteristics (Volume, Velocity, Variety, Veracity, Value)

In our digital age, data has evolved from being a mere resource to the lifeblood of organizations, governments, and individuals. The exponential growth in data generation has given rise to what we now call Big Data. This term encapsulates a set of defining characteristics that distinguish it from traditional data sources and pose unique challenges and opportunities. The five key characteristics of Big Data are volume, velocity, variety, veracity, and value.

At the heart of Big Data lies its sheer volume. It's not just big; it's massive, often exceeding the storage capacities and processing capabilities of conventional data management systems. Big Data encompasses datasets that range from terabytes to petabytes and even exabytes. To put this into perspective, a single exabyte is equivalent to one quintillion bytes, or one billion gigabytes. This staggering volume is the result of data being generated from an ever-expanding array of sources, including sensors, social media, e-commerce transactions, and scientific instruments.

The volume of Big Data presents a significant challenge. Storing, managing, and processing such massive datasets require specialized infrastructure, including high-performance storage systems, distributed computing frameworks, and robust data centers. Organizations must invest in these technologies to leverage the insights hidden within the data deluge.

In the digital realm, data is not a static entity; it flows like a relentless torrent. This is where the velocity characteristic of Big Data comes into play. Data is generated and transmitted at an unprecedented pace, often in real-time or near-real-time. Social media updates, sensor readings, financial market data, and website clickstreams are just a few examples of data sources that produce continuous streams of information.

The velocity of Big Data challenges traditional data processing methods. It demands systems that can ingest, process, and analyze data on the fly. Real-time analytics and decision-making require technologies and algorithms capable of fast handling data streams. Businesses, for instance, need to react swiftly to market changes, while industries like healthcare benefit from monitoring patient data in real-time to enhance care delivery.

Data doesn't conform to a single, uniform structure. Instead, it comes in many formats, ranging from structured data, such as databases and spreadsheets, to unstructured or semi-structured data, including text documents, images, videos, and social media posts. This diversity is what defines the variety characteristic of Big Data.

Variety presents a considerable challenge because it requires organizations to integrate and analyze data from disparate sources and in various formats. Conventional databases and analytical tools are often ill-equipped to handle this diversity. To extract valuable insights from Big Data, organizations must employ flexible data integration techniques and advanced analytics capable of handling this heterogeneous landscape.

Veracity addresses the trustworthiness of data. In the realm of Big Data, data quality is a significant concern. With the vast amount of data being generated, its accuracy, completeness, and consistency is often uncertain. Data may contain errors, duplications, or inconsistencies, leading to incorrect conclusions and flawed decision-making.

Veracity challenges organizations to establish data quality assurance processes. This includes data validation, cleaning, and verification procedures to ensure that data is reliable and trustworthy. Addressing veracity is essential, as flawed data can have far-reaching consequences, from financial losses to reputational damage.

The ultimate goal of Big Data is to derive value from it. The value characteristic represents the potential insights, innovations, and benefits that can be extracted from Big Data when it is effectively analyzed and leveraged. This value can manifest in numerous ways, from optimizing business operations and improving customer experiences to driving scientific discoveries and innovations.

Organizations must invest in advanced analytics, machine learning, and data visualization tools to unlock value from Big Data. These technologies enable the discovery of patterns, correlations, and actionable insights within the data. Value also extends to societal benefits, such as improved healthcare outcomes, enhanced disaster prediction, and sustainable urban planning, where Big Data contributes to making our world a better place.

In conclusion, the characteristics of Big Data—volume, velocity, variety, veracity, and value—define the unique nature of the data landscape in our digital age. Organizations and individuals must understand and navigate these characteristics to harness the full potential of Big Data. It requires investment in technology, data governance, and analytical capabilities to address the challenges posed by the data deluge and to transform data into valuable insights and innovations. As we continue to generate and accumulate vast amounts of data, leveraging these characteristics becomes increasingly critical for decision-makers, researchers, and innovators across diverse domains and industries.

The Growth of Big Data

In the annals of human history, the 21st century will be remembered for technological advancements and the unprecedented growth of data. This data explosion, often called the "Big Data" phenomenon, has fundamentally reshaped how we live, work, and interact with the world. It is a story of staggering numbers, exponential growth, and profound implications. To understand the present and future of Big Data, it is imperative to trace its remarkable journey from its nascent beginnings to the pervasive force it has become today.

The seeds of Big Data were sown long before the term came into vogue. Data accumulation has a rich history dating back to the earliest human civilizations. Hieroglyphs, cuneiform script, and parchment manuscripts were the data storage media of ancient times. These records, from accounting to religious texts, served various purposes and were painstakingly preserved through generations.

As we go toward the industrial revolution, data generation significantly increases. Mechanized factories, transportation systems, and the proliferation of printed materials created torrents of data, albeit in forms quite different from what we recognize today. Nonetheless, these historical examples represent the embryonic stages of data accumulation, setting the stage for what was to come.

The true catalyst for the growth of Big Data arrived with the digital revolution. Data generation on a never-before-seen scale became possible with the acceleration of the shift from analog to digital technology in the second half of the 20th century. The invention of the computer, followed by the advent of the internet, paved the way for an explosion in digital data.

The 1980s and 1990s witnessed the birth of personal computing, the development of relational databases, and the rise of the World Wide Web. These technological milestones marked a shift from physical to digital data storage and transmission. Suddenly, data could be created, accessed, and shared globally with remarkable ease.

Data generation was changed by the Internet's advent as a global platform for communication. Email, websites, and online forums created new data sources, but the rise of social media in the 21st century truly transformed the landscape. Platforms like Facebook, Twitter, and Instagram encourage users to share their thoughts, photos, and experiences in real-time. As a result, an avalanche of user-generated content flooded the internet.

The "Web 2.0" era, characterized by interactive web applications and user-generated content, marked a pivotal moment in the growth of Big Data. Social media platforms became virtual data goldmines, collecting and storing vast amounts of user information, preferences, and behaviors. This data-fueled advertising and marketing and provided valuable insights into human behavior and societal trends.

As if the digital revolution and the rise of social media were not enough, the 21st century brought yet another data juggernaut: the Internet of Things (IoT). The term (IoT) describes a network of linked objects, sensors, and devices that can collect and exchange data. IoT devices have permeated every facet of our lives, from smart thermostats and wearable fitness trackers to industrial sensors and autonomous vehicles.

The proliferation of IoT devices has added an entirely new dimension to the growth of Big Data. These devices generate data continuously, often in real-time, and transmit it to centralized repositories or cloud platforms. The result is a constant stream of data from sources as diverse as household appliances, agricultural machinery, and urban infrastructure.

Big Data is not just a technological phenomenon but also a thriving industry. The potential for extracting valuable insights from data has spurred a multibillion-dollar market for data analytics, machine learning, and cloud computing services. Organizations of all sizes and across industries have recognized the strategic importance of data.

Companies like Google, Amazon, and Facebook have leveraged Big Data for their core businesses and have become pioneers in data management and analytics.

Cloud platforms, like the Amazon Web Services (AWS) and Microsoft Azure, offer scalable infrastructure for storing and processing Big Data.

Moreover, traditional industries have been transformed by data-driven approaches. Healthcare institutions use data analytics for diagnosis and treatment, financial institutions employ data for risk assessment, and retail businesses rely on data to personalize customer experiences. The ubiquity of data has shifted the competitive landscape, with data-driven decision-making becoming a key differentiator.

While the growth of Big Data has brought about remarkable opportunities, it has also posed significant challenges. The shes well as volume, velocity, and variety of data have overwhelmed traditional data management and analysis tools. Organizations grapple with the need for scalable infrastructure, data integration, and data quality assurance.

Data privacy and security have appeared as critical concerns. As more personal and sensitive data is collected and stored, the risk of breaches in data and privacy violations has escalated. Regulatory frameworks, like California Consumer Privacy Act and the General Data Protection Regulation, seek to address these concerns by placing legal requirements on data handling and protection.

Veracity, the trustworthiness of data, remains a persistent challenge. Data may contain inaccuracies, biases, or errors, leading to flawed insights and decisions. Ensuring data quality and reliability is an ongoing endeavor.

The journey of Big Data is far from over; it is just beginning. As technology continue to advance, we can expect even greater data generation, with the potential for new data sources we can scarcely imagine today. The growth of Big Data will continue to be driven by emerging technologies such as 5G networks, edge computing, and quantum computing.

AI and machine learning will be increasingly pivotal in making sense of Big Data. These technologies can uncover patterns, correlations, and insights that would be impossible to discern manually. As AI algorithms get more sophisticated, they will enable predictive and prescriptive analytics, offering decision-makers valuable foresight and recommendations.

The integration of Big Data and AI will fuel innovations across sectors. Healthcare will benefit from personalized treatment plans based on genetic and patient data. Transportation systems will optimize traffic flow and reduce congestion. Environmental monitoring will track climate change and natural disasters. These are just glimpses of the transformative potential of Big Data in the years to come.

The growth of Big Data is a testament to the ever-expanding capabilities of human technology and innovation. From its origins in ancient record-keeping to the present age of digital abundance, data has evolved into a dynamic force that shapes industries, drives decision-making, and influences our daily lives. It has brought about remarkable opportunities for innovation and progress while presenting formidable challenges.

As we stand on the cusp of an even more data-driven future, the responsible management and ethical use of Big Data will be paramount. Balancing the promise of data-driven insights with privacy, security, and bias concerns will be a defining challenge for society.

In the grand narrative of human progress, the growth of Big Data is a defining chapter that has and will continue to transform how we understand and interact with our world. It is a testament to our boundless curiosity, ingenuity, and capacity for adaptation in the face of a data-rich future that holds both immense promise and profound responsibility.

Challenges Posed by Big Data

The rise of Big Data has ushered in a new era of possibilities and opportunities, revolutionizing industries, enabling data-driven decision-making, and driving innovation. Yet, beneath the promise of Big Data lies a complex landscape rife with challenges. Data's sheer volume, velocity, variety, and veracity create formidable obstacles for organizations and individuals seeking to harness its potential. In this section, we delve into the multifaceted challenges Big Data poses, exploring the technical, ethical, and strategic issues that define the data-driven landscape.

The most apparent challenge of Big Data is its sheer volume. The data generated daily—whether through social media interactions, sensor readings, or e-commerce transactions—far surpasses conventional systems' storage capacities and processing capabilities. Petabytes and exabytes of data are now commonplace, necessitating a fundamental shift in data storage and management.

Traditional relational databases, designed for structured data, struggle to handle the massive amounts of unstructured and semi-structured data that characterize Big Data. As a result, organizations must invest in scalable storage solutions and distributed computing frameworks to accommodate the growing data deluge.

Cloud computing platforms including Amazon Web Services (AWS) and Google Cloud offer scalable storage and processing resources that can adapt to fluctuating data volumes, providing a solution to the volume challenge.

The velocity at which data is generated and must be processed presents another significant challenge. Data streams in real-time from social media updates, financial market data, and sensor readings. Organizations increasingly require real-time or near-real-time analysis to make timely decisions and respond to dynamic events.

Traditional batch processing systems, which analyze data in static datasets, fall short in the face of the velocity of Big Data. To meet this challenge, organizations turn to stream processing technologies like Apache Kafka and Apache Flink, which enable continuous data analysis as it flows. Real-time analytics, powered by these technologies, offer valuable insights for applications ranging from fraud detection to supply chain optimization. Variety, the diverse nature of data, adds complexity to Big Data. Data comes in various formats, from structured data in databases to unstructured data in documents and multimedia. Integrating, analyzing, and deriving insights from this heterogeneous landscape is formidable.

Data integration challenges stem from the need to harmonize data from disparate sources. Data scientists and engineers must navigate the intricacies of data transformation, schema mapping, and data cleansing. Emerging technologies like data lakes and data warehouses provide centralized repositories for diverse data types, simplifying the integration process. Additionally, tools like Apache Nifi and Talend offer data ingestion, transformation, and integration solutions.

The veracity characteristic of Big Data concerns the trustworthiness of data. With the vast amount of data being generated, there is often uncertainty about its accuracy, completeness, and reliability. Data may contain errors, biases, or inconsistencies, leading to incorrect conclusions and flawed decision-making.

Ensuring data quality is a persistent challenge in the Big Data landscape. Organizations must implement data quality assurance processes, including data validation, cleaning, and verification. Data governance frameworks and data quality tools are essential components of a robust data strategy. Data lineage and auditing capabilities help track data from its source to its consumption, promoting transparency and trust in the data.

The growth of Big Data has brought about heightened concerns regarding data security and privacy. As organizations collect and store huge amounts of personal and sensitive information, the risk of data breaches and privacy violations has escalated. The consequences of data breaches extend beyond financial losses to reputational damage and legal ramifications.

Regulatory frameworks, like the GDPR (also known as General Data Protection Regulation) and the CCPA (also known as California Consumer Privacy Act), have introduced stringent data protection and privacy requirements. Compliance with these regulations or laws is a legal obligation and a matter of ethical responsibility. Organizations must invest in robust cybersecurity measures, encryption, access controls, and privacy-preserving technologies to safeguard sensitive data.

Beyond legal compliance, ethical considerations in Big Data are gaining prominence. The power of data analytics and machine learning can be used to influence behavior, manipulate opinions, and perpetuate bias. The ethical use of data encompasses transparency, fairness, and responsible data stewardship.

The issue of bias in data and algorithms is particularly thorny. Biased data can perpetuate discrimination and inequality when used to train machine learning models. Addressing bias requires careful data selection, preprocessing, and model evaluation. Fairness-aware algorithms and ethical data collection and analysis guidelines are emerging to mitigate these concerns.

While the cloud offers scalable solutions, the resources required for Big Data projects can be substantial. Organizations must consider the costs associated with data storage, processing, and analytics tools. The challenge is to optimize resource allocation to balance performance with affordability.

Resource constraints extend beyond financial considerations. Skilled data scientists, engineers, and analysts are in high demand, leading to a talent shortage in the field of Big Data. Organizations must compete for top talent, invest in training, and develop strategies for retaining expertise.

Effective decision-making in the realm of Big Data requires a strategic approach. Organizations must define clear objectives and priorities for their data initiatives. They must align data efforts with broader business goals and ensure data investments translate into tangible value.

Data governance is integral to navigating these challenges. It involves defining policies, processes, and responsibilities for data management, privacy, and security. Data governance frameworks, data catalogs, and data lineage tools help organizations establish a structured approach to data governance. Collaboration between IT, data, and business teams is essential to ensure data efforts align with organizational strategies.

The challenges posed by Big Data are multifaceted and ever-evolving. While data's volume, velocity, variety, veracity, and value offer tremendous potential, they also demand innovative solutions and responsible practices. Organizations must grapple with technical complexities, ethical considerations, and resource constraints as they embark on their data-driven journeys.

In navigating these challenges, organizations that prioritize data quality, security, and ethics will be better equipped to harness the full potential of Big Data. Collaboration between data scientists, engineers, and business leaders is essential to align data efforts with strategic goals. As the Big Data landscape continues to evolve, the ability to address these challenges will be a defining factor in the success of organizations and the responsible use of data in a data-rich world.

CHAPTER II

Foundations of Data Science

What is Data Science?

In the digital age, we immerse ourselves in an ocean of data. Every click, transaction, sensor reading, and social media post generates information that, when harnessed effectively, can unlock valuable insights, drive innovation, and transform industries. Data science is the discipline that enables us to navigate this vast sea of data, extract meaning from it, and make informed decisions that shape the future. It is an interdisciplinary field that combines domain expertise, computer science, statistics, and critical thinking skills. This section delves into the essence of data science, its key components, and its transformative role in our data-driven world.

Data science is fundamentally the art and science of gaining insight and understanding from data. It marries statistical techniques and computational tools with domain expertise to uncover patterns, correlations, and trends within datasets. Data scientists are the explorers of this digital frontier, equipped with the skills to collect, clean, analyze, and visualize data, transforming it into actionable intelligence.

Data science operates at the intersection of three fundamental components: data, algorithms, and domain knowledge. Data is the raw material—a treasure trove of information in various forms, from structured data in databases to unstructured text, images, and sensor readings. Algorithms are the computational techniques that process and analyze data, revealing hidden patterns.

Domain knowledge provides context and expertise, guiding data scientists in framing questions, interpreting results, and applying insights to real-world problems.

The journey of data science follows a structured lifecycle.

It begins with data collection, where relevant data is gathered from various sources, including databases, APIs, and sensors. Data cleaning and preprocessing come next, involving tasks such as handling missing values, removing outliers, and converting data into a suitable format for analysis.

Exploratory data analysis (EDA) is a crucial phase where data scientists explore the dataset, generate summary statistics, and create visualizations to understand its characteristics. EDA helps identify patterns, anomalies, and potential hypotheses for further investigation.

The heart of data science lies in modeling and analysis. This phase involves selecting appropriate algorithms, building predictive or descriptive models, and fine-tuning them for optimal performance. Machine learning, a subset of data science, plays a pivotal role here, encompassing techniques for classification, regression, clustering, and more.

Once developed, models are validated and tested on new data to assess their accuracy and generalization capabilities. Model evaluation is essential to ensure that the insights drawn from the data are reliable and robust.

The final stages of the data science lifecycle involve deploying models into production systems and monitoring their performance over time. Continuous monitoring and refinement of models ensure that they remain effective as data evolves.

Data science relies on a toolbox of specialized software and programming languages. Python and R are popular programming languages for data science, offering a rich ecosystem of libraries and frameworks for data manipulation, analysis, and visualization. Jupyter notebooks offer an interactive environment for developing and documenting data science projects.

Libraries like scikit-learn, TensorFlow, and PyTorch offer various algorithms and tools for machine learning tasks. These libraries enable data scientists to build and train models for tasks like image recognition, natural language processing, and recommendation systems.

Data visualization tools like Matplotlib, Seaborn, and Tableau help transform data into visual insights, making it easier to communicate findings to stakeholders. Business intelligence platforms like the Power BI and Tableau also create interactive dashboards for data-driven decision-making.

The applications of data science span across industries and domains. In healthcare, data science predicts disease outbreaks, personalizes treatment plans, and analyzes medical imaging data for diagnosis. In finance, it's used for fraud detection, algorithmic trading, and credit risk assessment. In marketing, data science powers recommendation engines, customer segmentation, and A/B testing.

Data science is also vital in improving customer experiences. E-commerce platforms leverage data to offer personalized product recommendations while streaming services use algorithms to suggest content based on user preferences. Ride-sharing companies optimize routes and pricing through data-driven algorithms.

In environmental science, data science aids in climate modeling, ecological monitoring, and conservation efforts. Governments use data science to analyze census data, optimize public transportation, and enhance public safety through predictive policing.

With great power comes great responsibility, and data science is no exception. The ethical use of data is a critical consideration. Data scientists must adhere to principles of privacy, consent, and fairness. Handling sensitive information requires safeguarding against data breaches and protecting individual privacy rights.

Bias in data and algorithms is another ethical concern. Biased data can perpetuate discrimination and inequality when used to train machine learning models. To address this issue, data scientists must actively work to identify and mitigate bias in both data collection and model development.

Transparency and accountability are essential in data science. Documenting data sources, data processing steps, and model decisions is vital to ensure that results are reproducible and interpretable.

As technology advances, the future of data science holds exciting possibilities. Emerging fields such as explainable AI aim to make machine learning models increasingly interpretable and transparent, addressing ethical concerns around black-box algorithms. Quantum computing offers the potential to solve complex problems at speeds unimaginable with classical computers, opening new frontiers in data analysis.

Integrating data science with other disciplines like biology, chemistry, and social sciences will foster interdisciplinary research and innovation. Data-driven approaches will continue transforming industries and shaping our understanding of the world.

In conclusion, data science is the art and science of turning data into knowledge. It empowers us to make data-driven decisions, solve complex problems, and drive innovation across diverse domains. As data becomes increasingly integral to our lives and society, the role of data science will continue to grow in importance, offering endless opportunities for exploration and discovery in our data-rich world.

The Data Science Lifecycle

In the era of data-driven decision-making, the data science lifecycle serves as a structured framework for transforming raw data into actionable insights. It is a systematic process that guides data scientists and analysts through data collection, exploration, modeling, and deployment stages. This section explores the intricacies of the data science lifecycle, highlighting its key phases, techniques, and significance in extracting valuable knowledge from the ever-expanding data pool.

The journey of the data science lifecycle begins with data collection—a process akin to embarking on a quest for valuable information. Data, the lifeblood of the entire endeavor, can originate from diverse sources, including databases, APIs, sensors, and user interactions. The initial challenge is to assemble the relevant data required to address a specific problem or answer a particular question.

Data collection demands meticulous planning and consideration of data quality. It involves defining the project's scope, identifying data sources, and devising strategies for data extraction. Organizations must also address legal and ethical considerations, such as obtaining consent for data collection and adhering to data privacy regulations like GDPR and CCPA.

Once data is gathered, it often resembles a rough diamond in the rough—full of potential but requiring refinement. The data cleaning and preprocessing phase involves transforming raw data into a usable format. This includes handling missing values, removing duplicates, and ensuring data consistency.

Data preprocessing also encompasses feature engineering, a crucial step in shaping the data for analysis. Feature engineering involves creating new variables or modifying existing ones to enhance the performance of machine learning models. Techniques like normalization and scaling are applied to ensure that data attributes are on a similar scale, preventing some features from dominating others during model training.

With cleaned and preprocessed data in hand, data scientists embark on an exploration of the dataset. This phase, exploratory data analysis (EDA), is akin to a detective unraveling a mystery. EDA involves generating summary statistics, visualizations, and descriptive insights to fully understand the data's characteristics.

Data scientists create histograms, scatter plots, box plots, and other visualizations to disclose patterns, trends, and outliers within the data. EDA not only helps in identifying potential hypotheses but also guides the selection of appropriate modeling techniques. It is a critical step in framing the right questions and setting the stage for subsequent analyses.

The modeling and analysis phase is at the heart of data science. It involves selecting and applying statistical and machine learning techniques to uncover meaningful insights from the data. Data scientists build predictive models for classification, regression, clustering, and recommendation tasks.

Choosing the suitable model is a crucial decision that depends on the nature of the problem and the data at hand. Linear regression may be ideal for predicting numerical values, while decision trees or neural networks might be preferable for classification tasks. Data scientists often employ cross-validation techniques to assess model performance and prevent overfitting, ensuring that the models generalize well to unseen data.

Feature selection and dimensionality reduction techniques help simplify models and improve their interpretability. Data scientists also fine-tune model hyperparameters to optimize performance. The modeling phase is iterative, requiring experimentation with different algorithms and strategies to achieve the best results.

Before deploying models into real-world applications, they must undergo rigorous evaluation and validation. Model evaluation assesses the performance of the trained models using metrics like accuracy, precision, recall, and F1-score. These metrics vary depending on the specific problem and goals of the analysis.

Validation involves testing the model on new, unseen data to ensure it generalizes well and produces reliable predictions. Cross-validation techniques like k-fold cross-validation help assess model stability and reliability. The validation phase also helps identify potential issues that may require further refinement, such as model bias, overfitting, or underfitting.

The insights derived from data analysis are most valuable when they can drive action and decision-making. The deployment phase involves integrating the models into production systems or applications, where they can provide real-time predictions or recommendations. For instance, an e-commerce platform may use a recommendation model to suggest products to customers during their online shopping experience.

Once deployed, models require continuous monitoring to ensure that they perform as expected in a changing data environment. Monitoring involves tracking model performance, detecting drift or degradation, and retraining models as necessary. It is an ongoing process that ensures models remain effective and reliable over time.

The data science lifecycle is an intricate journey—a quest for insights that begins with data collection and culminates in informed decision-making. It embodies the iterative nature of data science, where data scientists explore, model, validate, and deploy models to extract knowledge from data.

Each phase of the data science lifecycle is essential, from the meticulous data collection to the insightful exploratory data analysis, the modeling and analysis that uncovers patterns, and the validation and deployment that put those insights into action. Monitoring ensures that the journey continues, adapting to the evolving data landscape.

In a world awash with data, the data science lifecycle serves as a compass, guiding organizations and individuals through the complexities of data analysis. It empowers us to unravel the mysteries hidden within data, make data-driven decisions, and embark on a continuous odyssey of discovery and innovation in our data-rich world.

Role of Data Scientists

Data has become the lifeblood of organizations, governments, and industries in the digital age. The exponential growth in data generation has given rise to a pivotal role—the data scientist. These analytical wizards possess a unique skill set that enables them to extract insights from complex datasets, turning raw information into actionable knowledge. In this section, we explore the multifaceted role of data scientists, their responsibilities, and their impact on shaping our data-driven world.

At the core of the data scientist's role is problem-solving. Data scientists are the detectives of the digital age, tasked with solving intricate puzzles and answering questions that can drive business decisions, scientific discoveries, and societal advancements. They collaborate with stakeholders to define clear objectives and formulate research questions that data can address.

For example, in the healthcare industry, data scientists might work on predicting disease outbreaks, optimizing patient treatment plans, or analyzing medical imaging data for diagnostic purposes. In e-commerce, they can develop recommendation systems to personalize customer product suggestions. In finance, data scientists combat fraud and assess credit risk, while in transportation, they optimize routes and schedules.

One of the foundational responsibilities of data scientists is data collection and preparation. They source data from many places, including databases, APIs, web scraping, and sensors. This process requires selecting and gathering relevant datasets while adhering to legal and ethical considerations, such as data privacy regulations.

Once data is acquired, data scientists embark on the critical task of data cleaning and preprocessing. They remove duplicates, handle missing values, and transform data into a format suitable for analysis. This phase ensures the data is accurate and reliable for subsequent exploration and modeling.

Exploratory data analysis (EDA) is where data scientists unearth insights and patterns within the data. It involves generating summary statistics, creating visualizations, and conducting statistical tests to fully understand the data's characteristics. EDA helps identify anomalies, outliers, and potential hypotheses for further investigation.

Through data visualization tools and techniques, data scientists craft charts, graphs, and dashboards that reveal trends and relationships within the data. EDA is an iterative process that guides the selection of appropriate modeling techniques and informs the framing of research questions.

The heart of data science lies in modeling and analysis. Data scientists employ various statistical and machine learning techniques to build predictive and descriptive models. These models can be utilized for classification, regression, clustering, and recommendation tasks.

Selecting the right model depends on the nature of the problem and the data. For instance, linear regression may be suitable for predicting numerical values, while decision trees or neural networks might be preferable for classification tasks. Data scientists fine-tune model parameters, validate models, and assess their performance using accuracy, precision, and recall metrics.

They must undergo validation and deployment before models can make a real-world impact. Data scientists evaluate model performance on unseen data to ensure that it generalizes well and produces reliable predictions. Validation involves testing models for issues such as bias, overfitting, or underfitting.

Once validated, models are deployed into production systems or applications, where they can provide real-time predictions or recommendations. For example, an e-commerce platform might use a recommendation model to suggest products to users, enhancing their shopping experience.

Data science doesn't end with model deployment—it's an ongoing process. Data scientists monitor models to ensure they continue performing effectively as new data becomes available. Continuous monitoring involves tracking model performance, detecting drift or degradation, and retraining models as necessary.

Model refinement is another aspect of the data scientist's role. They continuously seek ways to improve model accuracy, efficiency, and interpretability. This iterative process ensures that models remain relevant and reliable in a dynamic data landscape.

Data scientists are not isolated experts but integral members of interdisciplinary teams. They collaborate with domain experts, business analysts, software engineers, and other stakeholders to translate data-driven insights into actionable strategies. Effective communication is key, as data scientists must convey complex findings comprehensibly to nontechnical audiences.

In interdisciplinary collaborations, data scientists often bridge the gap between data and domain knowledge. For example, in genomics, data scientists work alongside geneticists to analyze vast genomic datasets and identify potential links between genes and diseases.

Ethical considerations loom large in the role of data scientists. They handle sensitive and often personal data, necessitating a commitment to privacy, consent, and transparency. Data scientists must ensure that their analyses do not perpetuate bias or discrimination, particularly in machine learning models.

Addressing bias is a critical ethical challenge. Biased data can lead to biased models, with far-reaching consequences. Data scientists must actively work to identify and mitigate bias in data collection, preprocessing, and modeling. Ethical guidelines, fairness-aware algorithms, and transparent documentation are emerging tools to help navigate these challenges.

Data scientists' role is evolving with technological advances and data's growing importance in decision-making. Explainable AI, for instance, aims to make machine learning models more interpretable, addressing concerns about black-box algorithms. Integrating data science with other fields, such as biology, physics, and social sciences, fosters interdisciplinary research and innovation.

Quantum computing represents another frontier in data science. Complex problems could be solved by quantum computers at speeds that are not possible for classical computers. This technology opens new avenues for data analysis and simulation, with applications in cryptography, drug discovery, and climate modeling.

In a world inundated with data, data scientists serve as navigators, guiding organizations through data analysis and interpretation complexities. They are the architects of data-driven decision-making, transforming raw data into actionable knowledge. With their analytical skills, domain expertise, and ethical responsibility, data scientists play an indispensable role in shaping our data-driven future, unlocking insights, driving innovation, and addressing the challenges of our increasingly complex and data-rich world.

Essential Skills for Data Scientists

The role of a data scientist is one of the most sought-after and dynamic positions in the modern workforce. These professionals are instrumental in turning raw data into actionable insights that drive decision-making and innovation. To excel in this role and meet the demands of an ever-evolving data landscape, data scientists must possess diverse essential skills. This section delves into these critical skills that empower data scientists to navigate the data-driven landscape effectively.

At the core of a data scientist's toolkit lies programming proficiency. Data scientists commonly use programming languages like Python and R for data manipulation, analysis, and model development. These languages provide extensive libraries and packages tailored to data science tasks. Proficiency in coding enables data scientists to clean, preprocess, and transform data efficiently, making it ready for analysis.

A deep understanding of statistics and mathematics is fundamental to the work of data scientists. They apply statistical techniques to explore data, test hypotheses, and build predictive models. Concepts like probability, hypothesis testing, regression analysis, and linear algebra underpin their ability to derive meaningful insights and make data-driven decisions.

Effective communication is a linchpin skill for data scientists. They must convey complex findings to diverse audiences, including non-technical stakeholders. Data visualization is pivotal in this regard, allowing data scientists to present insights clearly and compellingly. Proficiency in tools like Matplotlib, Seaborn, or Tableau enables data scientists to create informative visualizations that facilitate understanding and decision-making.

To extract significant insights from data, data scientists must have domain knowledge related to their industry or field. Whether it's healthcare, finance, marketing, or any other domain, understanding the context and nuances of the subject matter is crucial. Domain knowledge guides data scientists in formulating relevant research questions and interpreting data in a meaningful context.

Machine learning is a cornerstone of data science, allowing data scientists to build predictive and prescriptive models. Proficiency in machine learning algorithms, such as decision trees, support vector machines, and neural networks, empowers data scientists to develop models that can make forecasts, classify data, or cluster information. Knowledge of model evaluation techniques and hyperparameter tuning is essential for building effective models.

In an era of big data, data scientists often encounter massive datasets that require specialized tools and technologies for analysis. Familiarity with big data technologies including Hadoop, Spark, and distributed computing frameworks is crucial. These technologies enable data scientists to process and analyze large volumes of data efficiently, unlocking insights that might be otherwise elusive.

With excellent data power comes great responsibility. Data scientists must adhere to ethical principles and data privacy regulations. Understanding the ethical considerations of data collection, handling, and analysis is essential. Data scientists should be vigilant in ensuring that their work does not perpetuate bias or discrimination and should actively work to mitigate bias in both data and models.

Data scientists are problem solvers at their core. They should possess strong analytical and critical thinking skills to frame research questions, design experiments, and troubleshoot challenges that arise during data analysis. The ability to think critically and adapt to evolving data landscapes is invaluable.

The field of data science is dynamic, with new tools, techniques, and technologies emerging regularly. Data scientists must be dedicated to lifelong learning and flexibility. Maintaining current knowledge of the most recent developments in data science, machine learning, and big data is crucial for professionals to be competitive and productive in their roles.

Data science projects often involve interdisciplinary teams comprising data scientists, domain experts, engineers, and business analysts. Effective collaboration and teamwork skills are vital for successful project outcomes. Data scientists must be able to communicate their findings, work cohesively with team members, and integrate data-driven insights into organizational strategies.

In conclusion, data science is a multifaceted field that demands many skills. While technical expertise in programming, statistics, and machine learning is foundational, data scientists also require soft skills like communication, critical thinking, and adaptability. These essential skills empower data scientists to extract valuable insights from data, make informed decisions, and drive innovation in our data-driven world. Whether solving complex problems or uncovering hidden trends, data scientists are pivotal in shaping the future of industries and society through the transformative power of data.

CHAPTER III

Data Collection and Preparation

Data Collection Methods

In the information age, data collection methods serve as the foundational step in transforming raw data into actionable insights. The process of collecting data, whether through surveys, sensors, or web scraping, plays a pivotal role in research, decision-making, and innovation across diverse domains. This section explores various data collection methods, their applications, and the importance of selecting the right approach to gather high-quality data.

Surveys and questionnaires are classic data collection methods for gathering information from individuals or groups. They are employed in fields ranging from market research to social sciences. Surveys allow researchers to solicit respondents' opinions, preferences, and demographic data. Online surveys have become more popular due to their cost-effectiveness and ease of distribution.

Observational studies involve direct or indirect observation of subjects or phenomena. Researchers record behaviors, events, or conditions as they naturally occur. This method is valuable in fields like anthropology, ecology, and psychology. It provides unfiltered insights into real-world situations but requires careful design to avoid bias.

Interviews are in-depth conversations between researchers and participants. Qualitative research often uses them to gather detailed information, personal experiences, and insights. Structured interviews follow predefined questions, while semi-structured or unstructured interviews allow for open-ended discussions. Interviews are a powerful method for understanding complex human behaviors and motivations.

Experiments are controlled studies where researchers manipulate variables to observe their effects on outcomes. Controlled conditions allow for causal inferences, making experiments crucial in medicine and psychology. Data collected through experiments often include measurements, observations, or responses to stimuli.

In the Internet of Things (IoT) era, sensors play a pivotal role in data collection. Sensors can capture environmental data (e.g., temperature, humidity), physiological data (e.g., heart rate, blood pressure), and more. They are employed in environmental monitoring, healthcare, and smart cities, providing real-time insights into various phenomena.

Web scraping and crawling are methods used to extract data from websites and online sources. Automated bots or scripts navigate web pages, collect information, and store it for analysis. This method is indispensable in data journalism, competitive intelligence, and market research.

The proliferation of social media platforms has given rise to a vast amount of user-generated content. Researchers and organizations collect data from social media to gain insights into public opinion, sentiment analysis, and trends. Social media data is valuable for marketing, brand monitoring, and understanding online communities.

Remote sensing entails collecting data from a distance, typically using satellites or aerial platforms. It is widely used in earth sciences, agriculture, and environmental monitoring. Remote sensing provides valuable information about land use, climate, and natural disasters.

Government agencies and administrative bodies collect a wealth of data through various processes, such as censuses, surveys, and records. These datasets are often used for policy analysis, urban planning, and public health research. Access to administrative data can be essential for evidence-based decision-making.

The proliferation of mobile apps and wearables has democratized data collection. Mobile applications can collect data on users' location, health, and behavior. Wearable devices, such as fitness trackers, continuously monitor physiological data. These methods have transformed healthcare, fitness, and personal data tracking.

Selecting the appropriate data collection method is critical to the success of any research or data-driven project. The choice depends on the research objectives, the nature of the data, and ethical considerations. Researchers must consider factors like data quality, sample size, and potential bias.

Moreover, the chosen method must align with the research question. For instance, surveys and interviews may be suitable if the goal is to understand consumer preferences. Sensor data and remote sensing would be more appropriate if the aim is to monitor air quality in a city.

Ethical considerations, including consent, privacy, and data security, are paramount in data collection. Researchers must adhere to ethical guidelines and obtain informed consent when dealing with human subjects. Additionally, they should ensure the secure handling and storage of collected data to protect individuals' privacy.

In conclusion, data collection methods are the cornerstone of data-driven decision-making, research, and innovation. Each method offers unique advantages and limitations, making choosing the right approach for a given context essential. As the world becomes increasingly data-centric, the ability to collect, process, and analyze data effectively becomes a vital skill for organizations and individuals seeking to harness the power of information in our data-driven world.

Data Cleaning and Preprocessing

Data is often described as the lifeblood of the digital age, fueling innovation, insights, and decision-making across industries. However, before data can be harnessed to its full potential, it must undergo a crucial transformation: data cleaning and preprocessing. This essential step in the data science pipeline involves refining raw data, ensuring its quality, and preparing it for analysis. This section delves into the significance of data cleaning and preprocessing, its challenges, and the techniques employed to transform data into actionable insights.

Data is rarely perfect. Various issues, including missing values, inconsistencies, errors, and outliers can impair it. These imperfections can hamper the accuracy and reliability of analyses and models, leading to flawed insights and decisions. Data cleaning and preprocessing remedy these issues, ensuring that the data used for analysis is of high quality and integrity.

One of the most common challenges in data preprocessing is missing data. Missing values can arise for various reasons, such as data entry errors or survey non-responses. Handling missing data requires careful consideration. Data scientists must decide whether to remove records with missing values, impute values using statistical methods, or employ sophisticated techniques like multiple imputations.

Data points that considerably depart from the norm are called outliers. While they can sometimes indicate interesting insights or anomalies, they can skew statistical analyses and model performance. Data preprocessing involves detecting outliers through visualization and statistical tests and deciding whether to remove, transform, or cap extreme values.

Data transformation is another critical aspect of preprocessing. It involves converting data into a suitable format for analysis. Common transformations include scaling variables to have similar ranges, normalizing data to follow a specific distribution, and encoding categorical variables into numerical representations. These transformations ensure that data adheres to assumptions made by various statistical and machine learning algorithms.

Inconsistencies in data can occur when different sources or data entry practices are involved. For example, dates may be recorded in various formats, currencies may have different symbols, or units of measurement may differ. Data preprocessing includes standardizing formats, units, and representations to create a cohesive dataset.

Natural language processing as well as text mining present a distinct set of difficulties for data preprocessing. Text data often contains stop words, punctuation, and special characters that may not be relevant for analysis. Preprocessing steps include tokenization (breaking text into words or phrases), stemming (reducing words to their root form), and removing stopwords and special characters to focus on the meaningful content of the text.

Data scientists sometimes work with multiple datasets that need to be integrated or aggregated to create a unified dataset. This involves matching or merging records based on common identifiers or keys. Aggregation may also involve summarizing data, such as calculating averages, totals, or percentages, to create meaningful insights.

Data preprocessing can be labor-intensive, especially with large and complex datasets. Data scientists often use programming languages like Python or R, along with libraries and frameworks that offer automation for common preprocessing tasks to streamline this task. Workflow automation tools and data pipelines are also employed to ensure repeatability and scalability.

Data preprocessing is not a one-time task but rather an iterative process. As data analysis progresses, new insights may reveal the need for additional cleaning or transformation steps. Furthermore, data source or collection process changes may introduce new challenges. Thus, data scientists revisit and refine preprocessing steps throughout the project.

Data cleaning and preprocessing serve as the alchemical process of transforming raw data into a valuable resource for data scientists and analysts. Data preprocessing ensures that the data is of high quality and integrity by addressing missing values, handling outliers, standardizing formats, and more. It paves the way for accurate analyses, meaningful insights, and data-driven decision-making. In the fast-paced world of data science, refining the raw material of data into a precious resource is an indispensable skill, turning data into gold for those seeking to extract knowledge from the digital age's vast treasure trove of information.

Dealing with Missing Data

Dealing with missing data is a challenge that data scientists and analysts encounter regularly in data analysis. Missing data can occur for various reasons, from survey non-responses to data entry errors, and it has the ability to introduce bias and reduce the accuracy of analyses and models. In this section, we delve into the significance of addressing missing data, the techniques employed to handle it, and the impact of various approaches on data-driven insights.

Missing data is more than just an inconvenience; it can profoundly impact data analyses and decision-making. When left unaddressed, missing data can lead to biased results, reduce statistical power, and impede the generalization of findings. Understanding and addressing missing data is thus a critical step in the data analysis pipeline.

One straightforward method of handling missing data is listwise deletion, where entire cases (rows) containing missing values are removed from the dataset. While this approach is simple, it can result in significant data loss, reducing statistical power and potentially biasing the analysis if missing data is not random.

Imputation methods entail replacing missing values with estimated values. Mean imputation replaces missing values with the mean of the observed values for that variable, median imputation uses the median, and mode imputation employs the mode. These methods are simple but may distort data distributions and correlations.

Regression imputation is a more advanced technique that uses regression models to predict missing values based on other variables in the dataset. This method can provide more accurate imputations by considering relationships between variables. However, it assumes that the missing data is missing at random (also known as MAR) or missing completely at random (or MCAR).

Multiple imputation is a sophisticated approach that generates numerous imputed datasets, each with different imputed values. These datasets are analyzed separately, and the results are combined to account for uncertainty due to missing data. Multiple imputation is considered one of the most robust techniques for handling missing data, as it can accommodate various missing data mechanisms.

In some cases, domain knowledge can guide the imputation process. Subject-matter experts may suggest reasonable values for missing data based on contextual understanding. This approach can be valuable when the missing data is related to a specific domain or context. The

choice of missing data handling method can significantly impact the results of data analyses. Listwise deletion, for instance, can lead to reduced sample sizes and potentially biased estimates if the missing data is not missing at random. Mean imputation can artificially inflate or deflate summary statistics, affecting the interpretation of results. Regression imputation and multiple imputation, when applicable, tend to produce more accurate and less biased estimates.

Addressing missing data also has ethical dimensions. Researchers must be transparent about their chosen method and its potential impact on results. In cases where imputation is used, reporting the imputation model and parameters is essential, allowing others to replicate the process and understand its limitations.

Dealing with missing data is a crucial aspect of data analysis that influences the quality and reliability of results. While no single method is universally appropriate for all scenarios, understanding the implications of different missing data handling techniques is essential. Data scientists and analysts must carefully consider the nature of the data and the assumptions underlying their chosen approach. By addressing missing data effectively, they bridge the gaps in their analyses, ensuring that the data's insights are accurate and actionable. In the quest for data-driven decision-making, the treatment of missing data is vital in constructing a complete and reliable narrative from the wealth of information at hand.

Data Transformation Techniques

Data transformation is a fundamental step in the data preprocessing pipeline, where raw data is converted and manipulated to make it suitable for analysis. These techniques play a pivotal role in data science, enabling data scientists to uncover hidden patterns, reduce noise, and prepare data for modeling. This section explores various data transformation techniques, their significance, and their applications in data-driven decision-making.

Scaling and normalization are essential techniques for ensuring that numerical data attributes are on a similar scale. Scaling transforms variables to have a common range, often between 0 and 1, while normalization adjusts data to follow a specific distribution, such as a basic normal distribution with a standard deviation of 1 and a mean of 0. These techniques prevent larger-scale attributes from dominating analyses, especially in machine learning algorithms that rely on distance metrics.

Categorical variables represent discrete categories or labels rather than numeric values. To include these variables in data analysis, they must be encoded numerically. Common encoding techniques include one-hot encoding, where each category becomes a binary (0 or 1) column, and label encoding, which assigns a unique integer to each category. Careful encoding ensures that categorical variables contribute meaningfully to analyses without introducing bias.

Log transformation is employed when data is highly skewed, with a long tail of extreme values. Taking the logarithm of such data compresses the range, making it more symmetric and amenable to analysis. Log transformation is often used in finance, epidemiology, and other fields where data may exhibit exponential growth or decay.

Binning involves grouping continuous data into discrete intervals or bins. This technique simplifies complex data distributions and can disclose trends or patterns that may not be apparent in the original continuous data. Binning is particularly useful in data visualization and summarization.

Aggregation and grouping techniques consolidate data by summarizing values within groups or categories. For example, data can be aggregated by averaging values within a specific time frame, grouping sales data by month or year. Aggregation simplifies data analysis, reduces data volume, and allows for higher-level insights.

Feature engineering is creating new features (variables) from existing data attributes. This process often involves domain knowledge and creativity. Feature engineering can lead to more informative attributes that improve the performance of machine learning models. For instance, in natural language processing, features like word frequency or sentiment scores can be engineered from text data.

A dimensionality reduction method known principal component analysis (PCA) converts high-dimensional data into a lower-dimensional space while retaining as much variance as possible. This technique is valuable for reducing the computational complexity of analyses, visualizing data, and identifying essential patterns in multivariate datasets.

Time series data often exhibits trends, seasonality, and noise. Time series decomposition techniques aim to separate these components, allowing for a clearer understanding of underlying patterns. Decomposition methods like seasonal decomposition of time series (STL) extract trends, seasonal effects, and residuals from time series data.

Smoothing and filtering techniques are employed to remove noise and highlight underlying patterns in time series or signal data. Moving averages, exponential smoothing, and low-pass filters are methods used to smooth data. These techniques are common in signal processing, finance, and sensor data analysis.

Feature scaling techniques, such as min-max scaling and z-score normalization, ensure that features used in machine learning models have similar scales. Feature scaling is crucial for algorithms like gradient descent, k-means clustering, and support vector machines, which rely on distance measures between data points.

In conclusion, data transformation techniques are essential tools in the data scientist's toolkit, enabling the conversion of raw data into a format that is amenable to analysis and modeling. The choice of technique depends on the data's nature, the analysis's objectives, and domain-specific knowledge. Effective data transformation enhances the quality of insights derived from data, facilitates the discovery of meaningful patterns, and empowers data-driven decision-making in various applications across industries and disciplines.

CHAPTER IV

Exploratory Data Analysis

Importance of Exploratory Data Analysis (EDA)

A crucial first stage in the data analysis process is exploratory data analysis (EDA), which is looking through and visualizing data to fully comprehend its properties and uncover insights. EDA goes beyond mere statistical summaries and charts; it is an immersive process that allows data scientists and analysts to explore, question, and ultimately tell the story within the data. In this section, we delve into the significance of EDA, its key objectives, and role in driving informed decision-making in a data-driven world.

One of the primary goals of EDA is to understand the fundamental characteristics of the data. This includes examining data distributions, identifying central tendencies (e.g., mean, median, mode), and measuring dispersion (e.g., variance, standard deviation). Understanding data characteristics is crucial because it provides insights into data quality, potential outliers, and the suitability of statistical methods for analysis.

EDA involves visualizing data through various plots and charts, such as histograms, scatter plots, and box plots. These visualizations help identify patterns, trends, and anomalies within the data. Patterns may reveal relationships between variables, such as correlations or clusters, while anomalies can signal errors, outliers, or unexpected phenomena. Detecting patterns and anomalies is essential for hypothesis generation and data validation.

Not all variables are equally important in many data analysis and machine learning projects. EDA assists in feature selection by highlighting which variables will likely significantly impact the analysis or modeling task. Additionally, EDA can inspire feature engineering, creating new variables from existing ones to capture important information or relationships.

Statistical analyses and machine learning models often rely on certain assumptions about the data. EDA helps data scientists assess whether these assumptions hold true. For instance, a linear relationship between variables is assumed in linear regression. Data scientists can check this assumption through EDA by plotting variables and assessing linearity. If assumptions are violated, adjustments or alternative methods may be necessary.

Data quality is a critical aspect of any analysis. EDA uncovers issues related to data completeness, accuracy, and consistency. Missing values, duplicates, and data entry errors are common problems identified during EDA. Addressing data quality issues early in the analysis process is crucial to avoid biased or unreliable results.

Data points that considerably differ from the majority of the data are called outliers. EDA helps identify and understand outliers, which can substantially impact statistical analyses and modeling. Outliers may represent unique phenomena or errors in data collection. Deciding whether to remove, transform, or retain outliers depends on the context and objectives of the analysis.

EDA fosters the generation of hypotheses by revealing potential relationships or patterns in the data. For instance, EDA might uncover a correlation between ad spending and sales in marketing. This discovery could lead to the hypothesis that increasing ad spending drives higher sales. Subsequent analyses can test and validate such hypotheses, guiding strategic decision-making.

Effective data visualization is a cornerstone of EDA. Visualizations make data more accessible and understandable to both technical and non-technical stakeholders. EDA enables the selection of appropriate visualizations, such as heatmaps, time series plots, or geographic maps, to convey key insights effectively.

In an era where data-driven decision-making is paramount, EDA plays a pivotal role. It equips organizations and individuals with the insights and knowledge needed to make informed choices. EDA helps uncover actionable insights, mitigate risks, identify opportunities, and optimize strategies across various domains, from healthcare and finance to marketing and environmental science.

In conclusion, Exploratory Data Analysis is not merely a preliminary step in data analysis; it is a dynamic and indispensable process that unfolds the narrative within the data. EDA empowers data scientists and analysts to understand data characteristics, detect patterns and anomalies, assess data quality, generate hypotheses, and enhance data visualization. By revealing the hidden stories within data, EDA serves as the compass that guides data-driven decision-making, ensuring that organizations and individuals harness the full potential of data to thrive in a complex and interconnected world.

Descriptive Statistics

Descriptive statistics is a foundational branch of statistics that seeks to summarize and present data in a meaningful and informative way. It serves as the starting point in any data analysis journey, providing a clear and concise snapshot of the key characteristics of a dataset. In this section, we explore the importance of descriptive statistics, its essential components, and its role in simplifying complex data into understandable insights.

At its core, descriptive statistics aims to help us understand the fundamental characteristics of data. It goes beyond raw numbers and provides insights into the central tendencies of a dataset, such as the mean (average), median (middle value), and mode (most frequent value). These central tendencies offer a glimpse into the typical or representative value within the data.

Descriptive statistics also delves into the variability or spread of data. Measures like the range, variance, and standard deviation quantify how data points differ from each other. A small standard deviation, for instance, suggests that data points are nearly clustered around the mean, while a large standard deviation indicates greater dispersion.

Data can often be complex and multifaceted. Descriptive statistics includes various techniques to visualize data distributions. Histograms, box plots, and frequency distributions provide graphical representations that offer insights into the shape, spread, and skewness of the data. Visualizations make it easier to identify patterns, outliers, and potential areas of interest within the data.

Outliers are data points that differ significantly from the majority of data. Descriptive statistics helps in identifying and understanding outliers. The presence of outliers can impact the mean and standard deviation, making it essential to consider their potential influence on data interpretations.

Descriptive statistics extends beyond numerical data to summarize categorical variables. Frequency tables and bar charts are commonly used to present categorical data, showing the counts or proportions of each category. These summaries help in understanding the distribution of categorical variables, such as customer demographics or product categories.

In addition to summarizing individual datasets, descriptive statistics allows for comparisons between different groups or categories within the data. Comparative analysis may involve calculating and comparing means, medians, or proportions across groups. This helps in identifying disparities, trends, or patterns that may not be apparent when looking at data in isolation.

Descriptive statistics do more than just present numbers; they provide context and insight. They transform raw data into a form that is easily interpretable and communicable. By summarizing data characteristics and visualizing distributions, descriptive statistics help stakeholders, whether they are data scientists, business analysts, or decision-makers, to grasp the essence of the data quickly.

Descriptive statistics serve as a foundation for informed decision-making. When faced with complex datasets, decision-makers need concise summaries that highlight key trends or variations. Descriptive statistics simplify the decision-making process by distilling data down to its most essential components.

It's essential to approach descriptive statistics ethically and responsibly. Misleading or incomplete summaries can lead to incorrect conclusions or biased decisions. Data scientists and analysts must be transparent in their reporting, clearly stating the methods and assumptions used in generating descriptive statistics. Additionally, they should be vigilant about potential bias, especially when dealing with sensitive data.

Descriptive statistics is the gateway to data insight. It turns data from a mass of numbers into a comprehensible narrative that can be acted upon. By summarizing data characteristics, measuring variability, visualizing distributions, and facilitating comparisons, descriptive statistics empowers individuals and organizations to make knowledgeable decisions, identify trends, and derive valuable insights from data. It serves as the essential first step on the data analysis journey, illuminating the story within the data and setting the stage for more advanced analyses and deeper exploration of the data-driven world.

Data Visualization

Data visualization is a powerful tool that transcends the language of numbers, transforming complex datasets into easily comprehensible and visually engaging representations. In today's data-driven world, data visualization is more than just an aesthetic exercise; it is a critical aspect of data analysis and communication. In this section, we explore the significance of data visualization, its diverse applications, and its role in illuminating patterns, trends, and insights hidden within data.

Data, in its raw form, can be overwhelming and difficult to interpret. Data visualization takes this intricate information and presents it in a visual format, making it accessible to a broader audience. Charts, graphs, maps, and interactive dashboards are some of the ways in which data is transformed into meaningful visual representations. These visuals simplify complex information, allowing individuals, from data analysts to decision-makers, to grasp the essence of the data quickly.

One of the primary objectives of data visualization is to reveal patterns and trends within data. Line charts can highlight trends over time, scatter plots can show relationships between variables, and heatmaps can identify clusters and correlations. Data visualization empowers data scientists and analysts to explore data visually, enabling them to spot insights that might be missed through traditional numerical analysis alone.

Data-driven decision-making is a hallmark of successful organizations. Data visualization plays a pivotal role in this process by providing decision-makers with clear and actionable insights. When presented with visual data, decision-makers can make informed choices, allocate resources efficiently, and develop strategies that are grounded in empirical evidence. Data visualization closes the gap between data analysis and decision implementation.

Data visualization is not just about presenting data; it's about storytelling. Effective data visualization conveys a narrative, guiding the audience through a data-driven story. By carefully selecting visuals, annotations, and design elements, data visualizers can communicate the key messages and takeaways from the data. Storytelling with data engages the audience and makes data more memorable and impactful.

Data visualization also plays a role in democratizing data. It makes complex information accessible to a broader audience, including individuals without a deep understanding of statistics or data analysis. Visualizations can be used in educational settings, journalism, and public policy to convey important information to the general public. As data becomes increasingly prevalent in our daily lives, data literacy and the ability to interpret visualizations become valuable skills.

Modern data visualization tools and platforms offer interactivity, allowing users to explore data on their terms. Interactive dashboards, for example, enable users to filter data, drill down into details, and interact with visual elements. This level of engagement encourages exploration and empowers users to ask questions and seek answers within the data.

While data visualization is a powerful tool, it is not without its challenges. Misleading visualizations, incomplete data, and biased design choices can distort the narrative conveyed by data. Data visualizers must be aware of these challenges and adhere to ethical principles in their work. Transparency, honesty, and clarity in presenting data are essential to maintain the integrity of data visualizations.

With data growing at an exponential rate, data visualization provides clarity in the face of complexity in this day and age. It is a universal language that cuts through boundaries, helping people and businesses understand data and derive valuable insights. Data visualization empowers data scientists, analysts, and decision-makers to explore data, spot trends, and communicate findings effectively. As we continue to navigate the data-driven landscape, data visualization will play an increasingly central role in shaping how we understand and harness the vast reservoirs of information that surround us. It transforms data from mere numbers into a compelling story, illuminating the path to data-driven decisions and innovations that propel us forward in an increasingly data-centric world.

Identifying Patterns and Anomalies

Identifying patterns and anomalies within data is a crucial aspect of data analysis that holds the potential to unlock valuable insights, inform decision-making, and reveal hidden trends. Whether working with financial data, medical records, or sensor readings, the ability to discern meaningful patterns and detect anomalies is central to understanding the underlying structure of the data. In this section, we explore the importance of identifying patterns and anomalies, the techniques used for this purpose, and the far-reaching implications of this process in various domains.

Patterns in data represent recurring structures or behaviors that can be discerned through systematic analysis. These patterns are not limited to visual shapes or forms; they can manifest as trends, correlations, or regularities within the data. Identifying patterns enables data analysts to make predictions, recognize opportunities, and gain a deeper understanding of underlying processes.

Anomalies, on the other hand, are deviations or outliers from expected patterns. Anomalies can be indicative of errors, fraud, unusual events, or critical insights. Detecting anomalies is vital in fields like cybersecurity, fraud detection, and quality control, where identifying unusual behavior or events is paramount to ensuring the integrity and security of systems and processes.

Identifying patterns and anomalies often involves the use of data mining and machine learning techniques. Data mining encompasses a range of methods for discovering patterns within data, such as clustering, association rule mining, and classification. Machine learning algorithms, including supervised and unsupervised approaches, can automatically identify patterns and anomalies by learning from historical data and making predictions based on learned patterns.

Data visualization is a potent tool for identifying patterns and anomalies. Visual representations of data, including scatter plots, line charts, and heatmaps, can highlight trends and outliers that might not be apparent in raw data. Visualization tools enable data analysts to explore data interactively, providing a deeper understanding of underlying structures.

Identifying patterns and anomalies is vital in business and finance. In the stock market, for instance, analysts use technical analysis to determine patterns in price movements, helping traders make investment decisions. In credit card fraud detection, machine learning models analyze transaction data to identify unusual patterns that may indicate fraudulent activity.

In healthcare, identifying patterns and anomalies plays a critical role in early disease detection and patient care. Medical imaging techniques, like MRI and CT scans, rely on identifying abnormal patterns in images to diagnose conditions. Patient records and vital signs can be monitored for anomalous patterns, alerting healthcare professionals to potential issues.

Environmental scientists and engineers use sensor data to monitor various parameters like temperature, humidity, and pollution levels. Identifying patterns and anomalies in this data helps track climate change, detect pollution incidents, and ensure the safety of ecosystems and communities.

Identifying patterns and anomalies is not without challenges. False positives (incorrectly identifying anomalies) and false negatives (failing to identify anomalies) can have significant consequences. It is essential to strike a balance between sensitivity and specificity, taking into account the domain and the potential impact of errors. Moreover, ethical considerations must be addressed when identifying patterns and anomalies in sensitive data, such as personal information or medical records, to protect privacy and ensure responsible use of data.

Identifying patterns and anomalies is a multifaceted process that holds the key to valuable insights and informed decision-making across a wide range of domains. Whether it's uncovering hidden market trends, detecting fraudulent transactions, diagnosing medical conditions, or safeguarding the environment, the ability to discern patterns and anomalies empowers individuals and organizations to explore the complexities of a data-rich world. With advances in machine learning, data mining, and data visualization, the potential for discovering meaningful patterns and detecting anomalies continues to expand, offering new opportunities for innovation and discovery in the ever-evolving landscape of data analysis.

CHAPTER V

Machine Learning for Big Data

Introduction to Machine Learning

Within data science and technology, machine learning, a branch of artificial intelligence (AI), has become a disruptive force. It includes a collection of methods and algorithms that let computers learn from information and come to conclusions or predictions without needing to be explicitly programmed. As we stand at the intersection of data abundance and computational power, machine learning has become a driving force behind innovations in various fields. In this section, we explore the fundamental concepts of machine learning, its applications, and its profound impact on our data-driven world.

At its core, machine learning seeks to allow computers to learn from experience and enhance their performance over time. Unlike traditional programming, where rules and instructions are explicitly provided, machine learning systems rely on data to automatically discover patterns, relationships, and insights. This data-driven approach empowers machines to adapt and make informed decisions, making them well-suited for tasks that involve complex data or require continuous learning.

Machine learning can be categorized into several subtypes, each with its own objectives and methods. Supervised learning involves training a model on labeled data, where the correct outcomes are provided, enabling the model to make predictions or classifications. Unsupervised learning, conversely, deals with unlabeled data and focuses on identifying patterns or clusters within the data. Reinforcement learning revolves around agents that learn to make decisions by communicating with an environment, receiving rewards or penalties based on their actions.

Machine learning has found applications in a wide range of industries, from healthcare and finance to manufacturing and entertainment. In healthcare, it aids in disease diagnosis, drug discovery, and personalized treatment plans. In finance, machine learning models predict stock prices, detect fraud, and optimize trading strategies. In manufacturing, it enhances quality control and predictive maintenance. In entertainment, recommendation systems use machine learning to suggest movies, music, and products tailored to individual preferences.

Natural language processing (NLP) and computer vision are two prominent domains within machine learning. NLP focuses on enabling machines to understand, generate, and interact with human language. Applications include sentiment analysis, chatbots, language translation, and text summarization. Computer vision, on the other hand, empowers machines to interpret and process visual information. It underpins facial recognition, object detection, autonomous vehicles, and medical image analysis.

Owing to its capacity to handle complex, high-dimensional data, deep learning—a subset of machine learning—has become incredibly popular. AI neural networks, which are modeled after the architecture and operations of the human brain, form the foundation of this system. Deep learning models, often referred to as deep neural networks, excel in tasks such as image recognition, natural language understanding, and playing board games like chess and Go. Their hierarchical and layered architecture allows them to learn intricate features and representations from data.

Despite its tremendous potential, machine learning is not without challenges. Data quality, bias, interpretability, and security are among the issues that require careful consideration. Biased training data can lead to biased model predictions, and the "black-box" nature of some machine learning algorithms can hinder their transparency and accountability. Concerns like fairness, privacy, and the responsible application of AI in decision-making also raise ethical issues.

Machine learning is at the forefront of the data-driven revolution, offering the promise of enhanced automation, decision-making, and insights across diverse domains. Its ability to learn from data, adapt to changing circumstances, and tackle complex tasks has positioned it as a catalyst for innovation. As machine learning evolves, its applications will expand, its algorithms will become more sophisticated, and its integration into everyday life will become increasingly seamless. The journey of machine learning is not merely about automating tasks; it is about augmenting human capabilities, advancing our understanding of data, and shaping the future of technology and intelligence in a data-centric world.

Supervised Learning

Supervised learning stands as one of the foundational pillars of machine learning, enabling computers to learn and make predictions or decisions based on labeled data. It is a type of machine learning where the algorithm is trained on a dataset containing input-output pairs, allowing it to learn the mapping from inputs to outputs. This guided learning process has wide-ranging applications and has played a pivotal role in various domains, from natural language processing to image recognition. In this section, we delve into the core concepts of supervised learning, its methods, and its significant impact on our data-driven world.

Supervised learning operates within a well-defined framework: it starts with a labeled dataset, where each data point consists of both input features and corresponding output labels. The algorithm's objective is to learn a mapping function that can accurately predict or classify new, unseen data based on the patterns it has learned from the training data. This mapping function can take various forms, including regression models for continuous output prediction and classification models for discrete label assignment.

In regression tasks, supervised learning algorithms aim to predict a continuous numerical value or outcome. For example, predicting house prices based on features like square footage, number of bedrooms, and location is a regression problem. Linear regression, decision trees, as well as support vector machines are commonly used algorithms for regression tasks. These algorithms learn to capture the relationships between input features and the continuous target variable.

Classification, another core component of supervised learning, deals with assigning discrete labels or categories to data points. Examples include email spam detection (classifying emails as spam or not spam) and image recognition (categorizing images into different objects or classes). Common classification algorithms include logistic regression, decision trees, random forests, and deep neural networks.

In supervised learning, the training procedure entails modifying the model's parameters iteratively in order to reduce the discrepancy between the training dataset's actual labels and anticipated outputs. The process is directed by a loss function that measures the error of the model. The loss function that is selected depends on the particular job; for example, mean squared error is often used for regression and cross-entropy for classification.

To assess a model's performance, it is evaluated on a separate dataset known as the validation or test set. Metrics like mean absolute error (MAE) and mean squared error (MSE) are used for regression, while classification models are evaluated using metrics like accuracy, precision, recall, and F1-score. The goal is to develop models that generalize well to unseen data, avoiding overfitting (where the model memorizes the training data) and underfitting (where the model is too simplistic).

Supervised learning has a vast array of applications that span across industries. In healthcare, it aids in disease diagnosis, patient risk assessment, and treatment recommendation systems. In finance, it powers credit scoring models, fraud detection algorithms, and stock price predictions. In natural language processing, supervised learning is behind sentiment analysis, language translation, and chatbots that can hold conversations with users. In autonomous vehicles, it enables object detection and decision-making processes critical for safe navigation.

Supervised learning is not without its challenges. High-quality labeled data is often required for training, which can be costly and time-consuming to obtain. Additionally, models may suffer from bias if training data is unrepresentative or reflects human biases. Ethical considerations also arise in areas such as healthcare, where predictive models must be fair and avoid perpetuating existing biases in medical decision-making.

Supervised learning represents a guided journey to machine intelligence, where labeled data serves as the compass that directs algorithms toward making accurate predictions and classifications. Its versatility and wide-ranging applications have reshaped industries and transformed the way we interact with technology. As supervised learning techniques continue to evolve, fueled by advancements in deep learning and neural networks, their ability to make sense of complex data and drive informed decisions will become even more integral to our data-driven world. Whether in healthcare, finance, or countless other domains, supervised learning stands as a testament to the power of guided intelligence in the era of machine learning.

Unsupervised Learning

A branch of machine learning that explores the intrinsic patterns, relationships, and structures within data without explicit supervision or labeled output, is known as unsupervised learning. Unlike supervised learning, where algorithms are trained on labeled data to make predictions, unsupervised learning thrives in the absence of predefined outcomes. Instead, it seeks to discover inherent structures and groupings within the data, making it a powerful tool for tasks such as clustering, dimensionality reduction, and anomaly detection. In this section, we delve into the essence of unsupervised learning, its techniques, and its wide-ranging applications across various domains.

At the heart of unsupervised learning lies the idea of letting algorithms autonomously explore and uncover hidden patterns within data. It operates with datasets where only input features are provided, without corresponding output labels or target values. This inherent flexibility makes unsupervised learning well-suited for scenarios where the underlying structure of the data is unknown or needs to be revealed. It essentially allows data to speak for itself, providing valuable insights that might not be apparent through manual inspection or predefined labels.

One of the primary tasks of unsupervised learning is clustering, where data points are grouped into clusters or subgroups based on their similarities or shared characteristics. Clustering algorithms, like the K-means clustering and hierarchical clustering, aim to partition data into clusters that are internally cohesive and well- separated from one another. Applications range from customer segmentation in marketing to species identification in biology.

Another critical application of unsupervised learning is dimensionality reduction, which involves reducing the number of input features while preserving essential information. Principal Component Analysis (PCA) is a common technique used for dimensionality reduction. By transforming high-dimensional data into a lower-dimensional representation, dimensionality reduction simplifies data visualization, reduces computational complexity, and often enhances the interpretability of data.

Unsupervised learning also plays a crucial role in detection of anomaly, where the goal is to identify rare or uncommon data points that deviate significantly from the majority of data. Anomalies can signify errors, fraud, or critical insights. Techniques such as autoencoders and isolation forests are used to detect anomalies within datasets. This is essential in domains like cybersecurity, where detecting unusual network activities is paramount.

Unsupervised learning finds applications across a wide spectrum of domains. In natural language processing, topic modeling using techniques like Latent Dirichlet Allocation (LDA) uncovers latent topics within text corpora, aiding in content recommendation and document summarization. In image analysis, unsupervised learning can identify patterns within image data, allowing for image segmentation and object recognition. In recommendation systems, it helps group users or items with similar preferences, enabling personalized recommendations.

Unsupervised learning presents its own set of challenges, including the determination of the optimal number of clusters in clustering tasks and the interpretation of discovered patterns. Additionally, as with all machine learning, ethical considerations must be addressed. Biased data can lead to biased clustering or dimensionality reduction results, reinforcing existing biases in the data. It is crucial to be aware of these challenges and strive for fairness, transparency, and ethical use of unsupervised learning techniques.

Unsupervised learning is a voyage of discovery, where data itself becomes the guide to hidden structures and patterns. Its ability to reveal intrinsic data relationships has profound implications across diverse domains, from marketing and finance to healthcare and artificial intelligence. As unsupervised learning algorithms continue to evolve and adapt, they will continue to provide valuable insights, offering a deeper understanding of complex datasets and reshaping how we analyze and leverage data in our data-driven world. Unsupervised learning stands as a testament to the power of autonomous discovery and the potential for unlocking hidden knowledge within data.

Deep Learning and Neural Networks

A subset of machine learning that has rapidly emerged as a driving force in the field of artificial intelligence (AI), revolutionizing how computers perceive, learn, and make decisions, is known as deep learning. Deep learning is centered around artificial neural networks, computational constructs inspired by the human brain's neural architecture. These networks excel at handling complex, high-dimensional data, making them instrumental in tasks such as image recognition, natural language processing, and autonomous decision-making. In this section, we delve into the world of deep learning and neural networks, exploring their fundamental principles, their applications, and their profound impact on reshaping AI.

Deep learning represents a paradigm shift in machine learning, characterized by the use of deep neural networks with multiple layers (hence the term "deep"). These networks, known as deep neural networks, are designed to automatically learn hierarchical representations of data. Each layer of a neural network processes data in a progressively abstract manner, with each subsequent layer building upon the representations learned by the previous ones. This hierarchical approach allows deep neural networks to capture intricate features and patterns within complex datasets.

At the heart of deep learning are artificial neural networks, computational models inspired by the interconnected neurons of the human brain. Neural networks consist of layers of nodes, called neurons or units, which are organized into an input layer, a hidden layers of one or more, and an output layer. Connections between neurons, represented by weights, enable information to flow through the network. During training, these weights are adjusted iteratively to reduce the difference between predicted and actual outcomes, allowing the network to learn complex mappings from inputs to outputs.

Convolutional Neural Networks (CNNs) have revolutionized image analysis tasks, like image classification and object detection. CNNs are designed to automatically learn and extract relevant features from images, enabling them to recognize patterns at different levels of abstraction. They leverage convolutional layers to apply filters that detect features like edges, textures, and shapes, followed by pooling layers for dimensionality reduction. CNNs have made remarkable strides in tasks ranging from facial recognition to medical image analysis.

Recurrent Neural Networks (RNNs) are tailored for sequential data, making them suitable for tasks involving sequences or time-series data, like natural language processing, speech recognition, and machine translation. RNNs incorporate feedback connections that allow them to maintain a hidden state, capturing information from previous time steps. This enables RNNs to model dependencies and relationships within sequences, making them effective in tasks like language modeling and sentiment analysis.

Deep learning has made substantial contributions to the field of Natural Language Processing (NLP). Models like recurrent neural networks (or RNNs) and transformers have transformed machine translation, text generation, and sentiment analysis. The introduction of large-scale pre-trained language models, like GPT-3 and BERT, has pushed the boundaries of NLP, enabling machines to understand context, semantics, and nuances in human language to an unprecedented degree.

While deep learning and neural networks have achieved remarkable success, they are not without challenges. Deep networks require substantial amounts of labeled data for training and are computationally intensive, often demanding specialized hardware like Graphics Processing Units (GPUs) and accelerators. Additionally, interpretability and transparency remain ongoing research areas, as deep networks can be viewed as "black boxes" with complex internal representations.

Deep learning and neural networks have reshaped the landscape of artificial intelligence, unlocking capabilities that were once considered beyond the reach of machines. Their ability to automatically learn intricate patterns from data has led to breakthroughs in image recognition, natural language understanding, and a myriad of other applications. As deep learning continues to evolve, with advances in architecture, training techniques, and model interpretability, its impact on our lives and industries will only grow. It represents a fundamental shift in how we approach AI, where machines learn not only to mimic human intelligence but also to perceive and understand the world in ways that were previously unimaginable. Deep learning and neural networks stand as a testament to the ability of AI to transform our data-driven future.

Choosing the Right Algorithm for Big Data

In the era of big data, where vast volumes of information flow continuously from various sources, choosing the right algorithm for data analysis is akin to charting a course through turbulent waters. The abundance of data brings both opportunities and challenges, as traditional algorithms may struggle to handle the sheer scale and complexity of these datasets. Selecting the appropriate algorithm becomes a critical decision, impacting the efficiency, accuracy, and scalability of data analytics. In this section, we explore the considerations and strategies for choosing the right algorithm in the realm of big data, acknowledging the multifaceted nature of this task.

Volume, Velocity, and Variety are the three Vs that define big data. Volume describes the vast amounts of data that are created and gathered, frequently more than conventional processing systems can handle. Velocity signifies the rapid rate at which data is generated, requiring real-time or near-real-time analysis. Variety encompasses the diverse types and formats of data, including structured, unstructured, and semi-structured data. These characteristics demand algorithms capable of handling the complexity and scale of big data.

To address the volume and velocity aspects of big data, algorithms need to leverage parallel processing and distributed computing. Parallel algorithms divide data into smaller chunks and process them concurrently, exploiting the power of multi-core processors and distributed computing clusters. Technologies like Apache Hadoop and Apache Spark offer frameworks that enable the parallel execution of algorithms on distributed systems, facilitating the processing of large datasets.

MapReduce, a programming model popularized by Google, has become a cornerstone in big data processing. It simplifies the development of parallel algorithms by breaking them down into map and reduce functions. These functions distribute tasks across multiple nodes in a cluster, processing data in parallel. MapReduce, along with its variants like Hadoop MapReduce and Spark, is suitable for tasks involving large-scale data processing, such as batch data processing and log analysis.

Machine learning algorithms are significant in extracting insights from big data. They can uncover patterns, make predictions, and automate decision-making processes. However, choosing the right machine learning algorithm for big data depends on various factors, including the nature of the data and the specific task. Algorithms like decision trees, random forests, and support vector machines are suitable for structured data, while deep learning algorithms, such as neural networks, excel in handling unstructured data like images and text.

In scenarios where real-time analysis of streaming data is essential, stream processing algorithms come into play. Technologies like Apache Kafka and Apache Flink enable the processing of data as it flows in real-time. These algorithms are vital for applications like fraud detection, sensor data analysis, and monitoring social media trends.

When selecting an algorithm for big data, considering scalability and resource requirements is crucial. Some algorithms may scale efficiently with the size of the dataset and available resources, while others may struggle or require extensive computational power. Evaluating the trade-offs between algorithm complexity, scalability, and resource utilization is essential for making informed decisions.

In practice, hybrid approaches and ensemble methods often yield the best results for big data analytics. Hybrid approaches combine multiple algorithms to leverage their strengths and mitigate their weaknesses. Ensemble methods, like bagging and boosting, combine the outputs of multiple algorithms to improve accuracy and robustness.

Choosing the right algorithm for big data is a multidimensional task that hinges on an understanding of data characteristics, processing requirements, and analytical goals. As the big data landscape continues to evolve, with the advent of new technologies and tools, the decision-making process becomes increasingly intricate. Successful navigation of this landscape requires a blend of expertise in data science, domain knowledge, and a willingness to adapt to the ever-changing seas of complexity. In the end, the right algorithm is not a fixed choice but an agile decision, tailored to the unique demands of each big data scenario, enabling organizations to extract valuable insights and chart their course towards data-driven success.

CHAPTER VI

Big Data Technologies

Overview of Big Data Technologies (Hadoop, Spark, etc.)

The advent of big data has transformed the way organizations collect, process, and derive insights from vast and complex datasets. To harness the potential of this data deluge, a suite of advanced technologies has emerged, each designed to address specific challenges in big data analytics. Two prominent players in this landscape are Apache Hadoop and Apache Spark, but they are just a part of a rich ecosystem of big data technologies. In this section, we provide an overview of these technologies, exploring how they enable organizations to manage, process, and analyze big data effectively.

Apache Hadoop, often referred to as the cornerstone of big data technologies, provides a robust and scalable framework for distributed storage and processing of large datasets. At its core, Hadoop consists of two key components: the Hadoop Distributed File System (HDFS) and the MapReduce programming model. HDFS stores data across a cluster of machines, ensuring fault tolerance and high availability. MapReduce enables parallel processing of data by dividing tasks into smaller subtasks and distributing them across the cluster. Hadoop's distributed computing model allows it to handle massive datasets by leveraging commodity hardware.

While MapReduce is a powerful paradigm, the Hadoop ecosystem has evolved to include a wide array of complementary technologies. Apache Hive provides a SQL-like query language for Hadoop, making it accessible to data analysts and SQL users. Apache Pig simplifies data processing tasks through a high-level scripting language. Apache HBase offers a NoSQL database for real-time, random read/write access to Hadoop data. Apache Spark, which we will discuss shortly, has become an essential component for in-memory data processing.

Apache Spark, often dubbed as the successor to MapReduce, has gained immense popularity for its speed, versatility, and ease of use. Spark extends beyond batch processing to support real-time stream processing, machine learning, and graph processing, among other tasks. One of Spark's standout features is its in-memory processing capability, which significantly accelerates data analysis by reducing disk I/O. Spark also provides high-level APIs in languages like Scala, Python, and R, making it accessible to a wide range of developers and data scientists.

Real-time data processing is a critical aspect of big data analytics, and Apache Kafka has emerged as a leading technology in this domain. Kafka serves as a distributed streaming platform that enables the ingestion, storage, and real-time processing of data streams. It acts as a highly durable and fault-tolerant event log, allowing applications to consume and produce data in real time. Kafka is widely used in use cases such as fraud detection, monitoring, and log aggregation.

Apache Flink is another stream processing framework that provides event time processing, exactly-once semantics, and stateful processing capabilities. It is well-suited for complex event processing and event-driven applications. Apache Cassandra, a distributed NoSQL database, is often used alongside big data technologies to handle massive amounts of structured and semi-structured data with high availability and scalability.

Machine learning is a crucial component of big data analytics, and a variety of machine learning libraries and frameworks have emerged. TensorFlow, developed by Google, is a powerful open-source machine learning framework known for its flexibility and scalability. Scikit-learn is a popular Python library that offers a wide range of machine learning algorithms and tools for data mining and analysis. These frameworks enable organizations to build and deploy machine learning models at scale for tasks like predictive analytics and recommendation systems.

Big data technologies have ushered in a new era of data-driven decision-making and insights generation. Organizations can now tap into the vast reservoirs of data at their disposal, thanks to technologies like Apache Hadoop, Apache Spark, Apache Kafka, and a plethora of other tools and frameworks. These technologies not only provide the infrastructure for storing and processing big data but also empower data professionals to build sophisticated analytics pipelines and machine learning models. As big data continues to evolve, organizations that embrace and master these technologies will be best positioned to thrive in an increasingly data-centric world.

Distributed Computing

Distributed computing stands as a cornerstone of the digital age, driving the vast infrastructure that underpins our modern world. This paradigm of computing extends beyond the boundaries of a single machine or data center, leveraging networks of interconnected computers to solve complex problems, process massive datasets, and deliver services at scale. Distributed computing has become the backbone of cloud computing, big data analytics, and the Internet of Things (IoT), enabling innovations that have transformed industries and redefined how we live and work.

At its core, distributed computing relies on the principles of parallelism and collaboration. Rather than relying on a single, monolithic system, distributed computing harnesses the collective power of multiple machines, often referred to as nodes or servers, to work together towards a common goal. These nodes communicate and coordinate their activities to achieve tasks that would be impractical or impossible for a single machine to handle.

Distributed systems come in various forms, each with its own architecture and design considerations. One common approach is the client-server model, where client machines make requests to centralized servers for resources or services. This architecture is prevalent in web applications, where web browsers (clients) interact with web servers to access websites and services.

Another architecture is peer-to-peer (P2P), where nodes in the network have equal status and collaborate directly with each other. P2P networks have been widely used for file sharing, content distribution, and decentralized applications (blockchain being a notable example).

Distributed computing offers several key advantages. First and foremost is scalability. By adding more machines to the network, distributed systems can handle increased workloads and data volumes. This scalability is essential for internet-scale services, social media platforms, and cloud-based applications.

Fault tolerance is another critical benefit. Distributed systems are designed to be resilient in the face of hardware failures or network disruptions. Redundancy and replication of data and services ensure that even if one node fails, the system can continue to operate, providing uninterrupted service.

Distributed computing finds applications across diverse domains. In cloud computing, providers like Amazon Web Services (AWS), Microsoft Azure, and Google Cloud Platform (GCP) leverage distributed systems to offer scalable and flexible infrastructure and services to businesses and developers worldwide. This enables organizations to run applications, store data, and process information without the need for extensive on-premises hardware.

Big data analytics relies heavily on distributed computing frameworks like Apache Hadoop and Apache Spark. These frameworks distribute data processing tasks across clusters of machines, enabling the efficient analysis of massive datasets. This capability has transformed industries such as finance, healthcare, and e-commerce, where data-driven insights are crucial.

While distributed computing offers remarkable advantages, it also presents challenges. Managing distributed systems can be complex, requiring expertise in network configuration, load balancing, and fault tolerance strategies. Ensuring data consistency and maintaining security across distributed environments are ongoing concerns. Additionally, debugging and diagnosing issues in distributed systems can be challenging due to their inherent complexity.

Distributed computing has propelled the digital revolution, enabling the development of powerful applications and services that have reshaped our world. From cloud computing to big data analytics and IoT, distributed systems are at the heart of the technological innovations that drive our daily lives. As technology continues to advance, the role of distributed computing will only become more pivotal, laying the foundation for the next wave of digital transformation and shaping the way we interact with data and information in the years to come.

Data Storage and Processing

In the digital age, data has emerged as one of the most valuable assets, and its effective storage and processing are the bedrock of modern information technology. The volume and variety of data generated daily are staggering, and organizations must employ sophisticated strategies and technologies to manage, store, and process this data efficiently and securely. In this section, we explore the essential concepts and technologies underpinning data storage and processing, from traditional databases to distributed file systems and cloud-based solutions.

Data storage involves the preservation of digital information for future retrieval and use. It encompasses various storage media and technologies, each with its own advantages and use cases. Traditional methods include hard disk drives (HDDs) and solid-state drives (SSDs) for on-premises storage. However, with the exponential growth of data, organizations have turned to network-attached storage (NAS) and storage area networks (SANs) for scalable and centralized storage solutions.

In recent years, cloud storage has gained immense popularity. Cloud providers like Amazon Web Services (AWS), Microsoft Azure, and Google Cloud offer scalable and cost-effective storage solutions that allow organizations to store and retrieve data on-demand. Cloud storage is particularly advantageous for its flexibility, accessibility, and the ability to accommodate varying storage needs.

Databases play a central role in data storage and processing. They are structured repositories that organize and manage data in a way that enables efficient retrieval, modification, and analysis. Relational databases, such as MySQL, PostgreSQL, and Oracle, use tables to store data in rows and columns, providing a structured format for relational data.

NoSQL databases, on the other hand, are designed to handle unstructured or semi-structured data. Document databases like MongoDB store data in flexible, JSON-like documents, while key-value stores, column-family stores, and graph databases cater to specific data models and use cases. NoSQL databases are often used in applications where data schemas evolve rapidly, such as social media and IoT.

In the era of big data, the storage of massive datasets has necessitated the development of distributed file systems. These systems distribute data across multiple servers or nodes, enabling scalability and fault tolerance. One of the most notable distributed file systems is Hadoop Distributed File System (HDFS), used in conjunction with Apache Hadoop for big data processing. HDFS divides data into blocks and replicates them across nodes, ensuring both data availability and reliability.

Data processing is the transformation of raw data into meaningful information. It encompasses a wide range of activities, from data cleaning and preprocessing to complex analytics and machine learning. Data processing pipelines often involve multiple stages, each tailored to a specific task.

Batch processing, exemplified by Apache Hadoop's MapReduce, is suitable for analyzing large datasets in a batch-oriented fashion. Real-time processing, on the other hand, is crucial for applications that require immediate insights, such as fraud detection or sensor data monitoring. Technologies like Apache Kafka and Apache Flink enable real-time data processing and stream analytics.

Cloud computing has reshaped the landscape of data storage and processing. Cloud providers offer managed database services, serverless computing, and machine learning platforms that abstract the complexities of infrastructure management. Organizations can leverage cloud-based solutions to scale their data storage and processing capabilities dynamically, paying only for the resources they consume.

While data storage and processing technologies offer immense opportunities, they also pose challenges. Data security, privacy, and compliance are paramount concerns, especially in light of stringent data protection regulations like GDPR and CCPA. Data governance and data quality assurance are essential to maintaining accurate and reliable data. Scalability, performance optimization, and cost management are ongoing considerations in managing data storage and processing solutions.

Data storage and processing are the unsung heroes of the digital age, enabling organizations to harness the power of data for innovation, decision-making, and insights generation. From the evolution of storage media to the emergence of cloud-based solutions, these technologies have continually adapted to meet the demands of the digital era. As data continues to grow in volume and complexity, data storage and processing will remain at the forefront of technological advancements, driving the digital future and shaping how we leverage data to address the challenges and opportunities of our rapidly changing world.

Streaming Data and Real-time Analytics

In the age of information, the velocity at which data is generated has reached unprecedented levels. From IoT sensors to social media updates, the constant influx of data is reshaping industries and business operations. To harness the value of this streaming data, organizations are turning to real-time analytics—a paradigm that allows them to process, analyze, and act upon data as it flows in real-time. In this section, we explore the significance of streaming data and the pivotal role that real-time analytics plays in unlocking actionable insights from this ever-growing torrent of information.

Streaming data refers to the continuous and high-velocity flow of data generated from various sources, such as sensors, applications, websites, and social media platforms. Unlike traditional batch processing, where data is collected and processed in fixed intervals, streaming data is ingested and analyzed as it is produced. This dynamic nature of streaming data offers businesses a real-time view of events and trends, enabling them to respond promptly to emerging situations and capitalize on opportunities.

Streaming data brings forth a unique set of challenges. The sheer volume of data can overwhelm traditional data processing systems, necessitating the use of specialized tools and technologies. Furthermore, streaming data is often noisy and may contain irrelevant or redundant information. The need for real-time processing introduces strict latency requirements, demanding efficient algorithms and infrastructure to ensure timely analysis. Finally, as data flows continuously, it may arrive out of order or with varying rates, making data integration and synchronization a complex task.

Real-time analytics is the practice of processing and analyzing streaming data as it arrives, extracting valuable insights, and taking actions in near real-time. This paradigm empowers organizations to make informed decisions, detect anomalies, and respond to critical events with minimal delay. Real-time analytics systems leverage various technologies, including stream processing frameworks, complex event processing (CEP) engines, and machine learning models, to analyze data as it is ingested.

The applications of streaming data and real-time analytics span a multitude of industries. In finance, real-time analytics are used for fraud detection, algorithmic trading, and risk management. In healthcare, streaming data from patient monitoring devices can trigger immediate alerts for medical professionals, potentially saving lives. In manufacturing, IoT sensors on machinery can provide real-time insights into equipment performance, enabling predictive maintenance and reducing downtime.

Several technologies and frameworks have emerged to address the challenges of streaming data. Apache Kafka, a distributed event streaming platform, is widely used for ingesting, storing, and processing real-time data streams. Apache Flink and Apache Spark Streaming offer stream processing capabilities, enabling the execution of complex analytics on data in motion. Cloud providers, such as AWS Kinesis and Azure Stream Analytics, offer managed streaming services that abstract the complexities of infrastructure management.

As data generation rates continue to soar, the importance of real-time analytics will only grow. The integration of artificial intelligence and machine learning into real-time analytics pipelines will enable organizations to derive more sophisticated insights from streaming data, from predictive maintenance in manufacturing to personalized recommendations in e-commerce. Additionally, the evolution of edge computing, where data is processed closer to the source, will further enhance the capabilities of real-time analytics.

Streaming data and real-time analytics represent a fundamental shift in how organizations harness the power of data. In a world where every moment counts, the ability to process and act upon data as it is generated is a competitive advantage that drives innovation and empowers data-driven decision-making. As technology continues to evolve, the potential applications of streaming data and real-time analytics are boundless, promising a future where organizations can ride the data stream to success in a rapidly changing world.

CHAPTER VII

Data Governance and Ethics

Data Privacy and Security

In an era defined by the relentless flow of data, data privacy and security have assumed paramount importance. The digital age has ushered in an unprecedented era of connectivity and convenience, but it has also brought forth profound challenges related to the protection of personal information, sensitive data, and critical systems. In this section, we delve into the critical concepts of data privacy and security, exploring their significance, challenges, and the evolving landscape of safeguarding our digital world.

Data privacy is the practice of controlling access to and usage of personal and sensitive information. In an increasingly interconnected world, individuals generate vast amounts of data, from their online behavior to personal identifiers like social security numbers and medical records. Protecting this data is crucial for preserving an individual's autonomy, rights, and dignity.

Data privacy is enshrined in various regulations and frameworks, the most notable being the General Data Protection Regulation (GDPR) in Europe and the California Consumer Privacy Act (CCPA) in the United States. These regulations require organizations to be transparent about their data practices, obtain consent for data processing, and provide individuals with the right to access, correct, or delete their data.

Data security focuses on protecting data from unauthorized access, breaches, and cyber threats. It encompasses a broad spectrum of measures and practices, including encryption, access controls, intrusion detection systems, and cybersecurity protocols. Data breaches can have severe consequences, ranging from financial losses and reputational damage to legal liabilities.

Cybersecurity threats continue to evolve, with hackers and malicious actors employing increasingly sophisticated techniques. Ransomware attacks, data breaches, and phishing attempts are commonplace, targeting organizations across industries. Therefore, robust cybersecurity measures are essential to safeguard sensitive data and critical systems.

Data privacy and security face numerous challenges in the digital age. One significant challenge is the sheer volume of data generated, stored, and transmitted daily. The proliferation of internet-connected devices and the rise of big data have expanded the attack surface, making it more challenging to secure data effectively.

Human factors also play a crucial role in data privacy and security. Insider threats, which involve employees or individuals with access to an organization's systems, can pose significant risks. Lack of awareness, negligence, and social engineering attacks can compromise data security.

Additionally, the global nature of data flows presents challenges in maintaining data privacy and security across international borders. Organizations must navigate the complexities of differing regulations and jurisdictions, which can vary significantly.

The landscape of data privacy and security is continually evolving to address new threats and technological advancements. Zero-trust security models, which assume that threats may exist both outside and inside an organization's network, are gaining traction. Artificial intelligence and machine learning are being harnessed to detect and respond to threats in real-time.

Privacy-enhancing technologies, such as differential privacy and homomorphic encryption, are being explored to protect data while enabling meaningful analysis. Blockchain technology is being leveraged for secure and transparent data sharing.

Data privacy and security are the cornerstones of trust in the digital world. As individuals and organizations continue to rely on data for communication, commerce, and innovation, the responsibility to protect this data becomes paramount. The evolving regulatory landscape, coupled with the ever-present threat of cyberattacks, underscores the need for vigilance and proactive measures in safeguarding data privacy and security. In this digital terrain, where data is the lifeblood of our interconnected society, the commitment to privacy and security is the key to a safer, more trustworthy, and resilient digital future.

Compliance with Regulations (e.g., GDPR, CCPA)

In an increasingly data-driven world, the protection of individuals' privacy and the secure handling of sensitive data have become paramount concerns. To address these issues, governments and regulatory bodies worldwide have introduced a slew of data protection and privacy regulations, the most notable of which are the General Data Protection Regulation (GDPR) in Europe and the California Consumer Privacy Act (CCPA) in the United States. In this section, we explore the significance of compliance with such regulations, the challenges it poses to organizations, and the evolving landscape of data protection.

The General Data Protection Regulation (GDPR), enacted in 2018, stands as one of the most comprehensive and far-reaching data protection regulations globally. It applies to any organization that processes the personal data of individuals within the European Union (EU), regardless of the organization's location. GDPR grants individuals greater control over their personal data, including the right to access, correct, and delete their information. It also imposes stringent requirements on organizations, mandating transparency in data practices, data breach reporting, and the appointment of data protection officers.

Compliance with the GDPR is a complex endeavor, necessitating a thorough understanding of data flows, data protection impact assessments, and the implementation of appropriate technical and organizational measures to protect data.

The California Consumer Privacy Act (CCPA), effective since 2020, represents a landmark in data protection legislation in the United States. It grants California residents certain rights over their personal information, such as the right to know what data is collected and the right to opt-out of the sale of their data. Similar to the GDPR, the CCPA places responsibilities on organizations, including the obligation to disclose data practices, maintain consumer requests, and implement security measures to safeguard personal information.

While the CCPA applies to California residents and businesses operating in California, its impact reaches beyond state borders. It has spurred discussions about the need for comprehensive federal data privacy legislation in the United States.

Achieving compliance with data protection regulations is a multifaceted challenge for organizations. The complexity of these regulations, coupled with the evolving nature of data technology, requires ongoing efforts.

Organizations must conduct thorough data audits, establish data protection policies and procedures, and invest in technology solutions to ensure compliance.

Another significant challenge is the need for organizations to adapt their data practices to accommodate varying regulations worldwide. Multinational companies face the daunting task of navigating the intricate web of data protection laws, each with its unique requirements and implications.

The landscape of data protection and privacy is continually evolving. New regulations, such as the California Privacy Rights Act (CPRA) and Brazil's General Data Protection Law (LGPD), have emerged. These regulations introduce additional requirements and rights for individuals, further emphasizing the global trend toward enhanced data protection.

Furthermore, discussions surrounding the privacy and security of emerging technologies like artificial intelligence and the Internet of Things have gained prominence. As these technologies become more integral to daily life and business operations, the need for comprehensive data protection frameworks becomes even more critical.

Compliance with data protection regulations is not merely a legal obligation; it is a commitment to respecting individuals' privacy and ensuring the secure handling of data. In an era where data breaches and privacy violations are increasingly prevalent, organizations must prioritize data protection to build trust with consumers and stakeholders. As the regulatory landscape continues to evolve and globalize, organizations that proactively address data protection concerns will not only meet their compliance requirements but also foster a culture of responsible data stewardship, setting the stage for a safer, more trustworthy digital future.

Ethical Considerations in Data Science

In the digital age, data science has emerged as a transformative force, powering innovations across industries and reshaping how organizations operate. Yet, with great power comes great responsibility, and the ethical implications of data science have come into sharp focus. Data scientists, organizations, and society at large are grappling with a host of ethical considerations, from data privacy and bias to accountability and transparency. In this section, we explore the multifaceted landscape of ethical considerations in data science, emphasizing the importance of a principled approach to technology-driven decision-making.

At the core of ethical data science lies the fundamental principle of data privacy and individual consent. The collection and use of personal data must be conducted with transparency and respect for individuals' rights. Data scientists must ensure that data is collected for legitimate purposes and only used in ways that are consistent with those purposes. Informed consent from data subjects is paramount, as individuals should have the right to control how their data is used and shared.

The introduction of regulations like the General Data Protection Regulation (GDPR) and the California Consumer Privacy Act (CCPA) reflects society's growing concerns about data privacy. These regulations empower individuals with rights such as the right to access their data, request its deletion, and be informed about data processing practices. Compliance with such regulations is not only a legal obligation but also an ethical imperative.

One of the most pressing ethical challenges in data science is the issue of algorithmic bias. Machine learning algorithms, when trained on biased data, can perpetuate and even exacerbate societal biases, leading to discriminatory outcomes. This can manifest in various domains, from biased hiring processes to unfair lending decisions and biased law enforcement practices.

To address algorithmic bias, data scientists must be diligent in dataset curation, ensuring that training data is diverse, representative, and free from biases. Additionally, ongoing monitoring and auditing of algorithmic outcomes are essential to detect and rectify biases. Developing ethical guidelines and best practices for algorithmic fairness is an ongoing endeavor within the data science community.

As machine learning models and algorithms become increasingly complex, the issue of transparency and accountability has gained prominence. Many advanced algorithms, such as deep neural networks, are often seen as "black boxes" where it is challenging to understand the rationale behind their decisions. This lack of transparency can hinder accountability and trust.

Ethical data scientists advocate for transparency in model development and decision-making. This includes documenting data preprocessing steps, model architectures, and evaluation metrics. Efforts are also underway to develop techniques for explaining model predictions, such as feature importance analysis and interpretable machine learning models.

Ethical considerations in data science go beyond theoretical discussions; they manifest in everyday practice. Organizations must foster a culture of ethical data science, where ethical principles are embedded into every stage of the data lifecycle, from data collection and processing to model development and deployment. This requires collaboration between data scientists, ethicists, and domain experts.

Furthermore, data scientists should remain vigilant in addressing emerging ethical challenges as technology evolves. Ethical considerations in areas like AI ethics, biometrics, and data sharing are continuously evolving and require ongoing attention and adaptation.

Data science has the potential to bring about transformative advancements, but it also carries significant ethical responsibilities. Ethical considerations in data science encompass data privacy, algorithmic bias, transparency, accountability, and more. Data scientists and organizations must navigate this complex landscape with a moral compass, ensuring that innovation is balanced with responsibility. As technology continues to shape our world, ethical data science is not merely a choice but an imperative—an imperative that reflects our commitment to respecting individual rights, promoting fairness, and upholding the ethical principles that underpin a just and equitable society.

Building a Data Governance Framework

In the age of big data, organizations are inundated with vast amounts of information that hold the potential for valuable insights and informed decision-making. However, this data deluge also brings forth significant challenges related to data quality, privacy, security, and compliance. To effectively manage and leverage their data assets, organizations must establish a robust data governance framework. This framework serves as a structured approach to defining policies, procedures, roles, and responsibilities for data management.

A comprehensive data governance framework includes several key components: data policies and procedures, data stewardship, data quality management, data privacy and security, data compliance, data catalogs and metadata, data ownership, data lifecycle management, and a data governance council or committee. These components collectively ensure that data is treated as a valuable organizational asset, maintained at high quality, and utilized effectively to achieve strategic objectives.

Implementing a data governance framework yields several significant benefits, including data quality improvement, privacy compliance, data security, efficiency, risk mitigation, enhanced collaboration, and the facilitation of data-driven decision-making. However, building a data governance framework is not a one-time effort but an ongoing process that involves assessment, defining objectives, engaging stakeholders, establishing policies, appointing data stewards, implementing technology, providing training and awareness, monitoring and measuring, and iterative refinement.

Despite the advantages, implementing a data governance framework presents challenges such as resistance to change, resource allocation, complexity, integration with legacy systems, and legal and compliance risks. Looking ahead, future trends in data governance may involve AI and automation for data governance tasks, blockchain for data integrity, decentralized data governance models, and the development of global data governance standards.

In conclusion, a well-structured data governance framework is imperative in the modern data-driven landscape. It empowers organizations to maximize the value of their data while mitigating risks associated with data quality, privacy, and compliance. Effective data governance aligns data management practices with organizational goals, fosters a culture of data responsibility, and positions the organization for success. Building and maintaining a robust data governance framework is an investment that pays dividends in data-driven insights, operational efficiency, and competitive advantage.

CHAPTER VIII

Extracting Insights from Big Data

Data Visualization and Dashboards

Data, in its raw form, can be overwhelming and incomprehensible. Data visualization and dashboards emerge as powerful tools in the data scientist's arsenal, transforming complex datasets into meaningful insights that can drive informed decision-making. This section explores the significance of data visualization and dashboards, their role in conveying information effectively, and their impact across various domains.

Data visualization is the process of representing data graphically, often through charts, graphs, maps, or other visual elements. At its core, it's about converting numbers and statistics into visual stories that are easier to understand and interpret. Visualization taps into our innate ability to process visual information rapidly, making it a potent means of communication.

One of the primary roles of data visualization is to facilitate effective communication. Whether it's presenting quarterly sales figures to stakeholders or conveying public health data to the general population, well-crafted visualizations can convey complex information succinctly and persuasively. This ability to distill data into comprehensible visual narratives empowers decision-makers to draw insights and take actions.

Data visualization helps uncover patterns, trends, and relationships in data that might go unnoticed in raw numbers or textual descriptions. By visualizing data, analysts and decision-makers can identify anomalies, correlations, and outliers, leading to more informed hypotheses and strategies. This is particularly valuable in fields like finance, where stock price movements are analyzed through candlestick charts, or epidemiology, where the spread of diseases is tracked through heatmaps.

Data visualization encompasses a wide range of techniques and types. Common visualizations include bar charts, line graphs, scatter plots, and pie charts. More advanced forms like heatmaps, treemaps, and network diagrams are used for specific data representation needs. Geographic information systems (GIS) allow for mapping data onto geographical landscapes, making it invaluable for applications such as urban planning and disaster response.

Interactive dashboards take data visualization a step further. These user-friendly interfaces enable users to interact with data in real-time, drilling down into specific details or adjusting parameters to explore different scenarios. Business intelligence tools like Tableau, Power BI, and QlikView have revolutionized decision-making by allowing organizations to create customized dashboards for tracking key performance indicators (KPIs) and visualizing data trends.

The applications of data visualization and dashboards are vast and extend across diverse domains. In healthcare, dashboards are used for patient monitoring and epidemiological tracking. In finance, real-time trading dashboards provide insights into market trends. E-commerce platforms leverage visualizations to optimize user experience and recommend products. Educational institutions use dashboards to monitor student performance and administrative operations.

While data visualization and dashboards are powerful tools, ethical considerations come into play. Misleading visualizations, such as truncated axes or distorted scales, can lead to inaccurate interpretations. Data privacy concerns must also be addressed, especially when sharing dashboards with sensitive information.

Data visualization and dashboards are not just tools for data scientists; they are vehicles for democratizing data and making it accessible to a wider audience. In an era characterized by data abundance, the ability to convey insights visually is indispensable. As technology advances, we can expect data visualization and dashboards to play an increasingly central role in our data-driven future. These tools will continue to bridge the gap between raw data and actionable insights, shaping the way we understand and interact with the vast world of information that surrounds us.

Predictive Analytics

Predictive analytics, a powerful branch of data science, has revolutionized the way organizations make decisions by forecasting outcomes in the future based on historical data and statistical algorithms. In this section, we explore the significance of predictive analytics, its methodologies, and the myriad applications across industries, all of which empower businesses and institutions to proactively respond to emerging trends and make data-driven decisions.

Predictive analytics leverages historical data to uncover patterns, relationships, and trends. By utilizing statistical models as well as machine learning algorithms, it predicts future events or outcomes with a high degree of accuracy. Essentially, it provides a glimpse into the future, enabling organizations to make proactive and informed choices.

Predictive analytics encompasses a range of methodologies, each suited to specific tasks. Regression analysis, for example, explores relationships between variables and is used for predicting numerical outcomes. Classification algorithms, including decision trees and support vector machines, are employed to categorize data into classes. Time series analysis is crucial for predicting future values based on past observations, making it indispensable in finance, economics, and meteorology.

Machine learning, with its versatile algorithms and capacity to handle large datasets, has become the driving force behind predictive analytics. Algorithms like linear and logistic regression, random forests, neural networks, and gradient boosting are routinely used for various prediction tasks.

Predictive analytics has applications across numerous domains. In healthcare, it aids in disease diagnosis and patient risk assessment, enabling timely interventions. In finance, it's used for credit scoring, fraud detection, and stock price forecasting. In marketing, predictive analytics assists in customer segmentation, churn prediction, and campaign optimization. Supply chain management benefits from predictive analytics by optimizing inventory levels and demand forecasting.

Predictive analytics is a vital component of modern business intelligence (BI) systems. Organizations use BI platforms to create interactive dashboards and reports, incorporating predictive models to support decision-making. Executives and managers rely on these tools to monitor key performance indicators (KPIs) and anticipate future trends, empowering them to adjust strategies in real-time.

While predictive analytics offers remarkable advantages, it's not without challenges. Data quality and data preprocessing are critical, as inaccurate or insufficient data can lead to flawed predictions. Ensuring fairness and addressing biases in predictive models is an ongoing concern. Ethical considerations, like data privacy and consent, must be addressed to protect individuals' rights and maintain trust.

The future of predictive analytics holds immense promise. As data sources continue to expand, including IoT devices and sensor networks, predictive models will gain even more accuracy and granularity. Explainable AI (XAI) is emerging as an area of focus, aiming to make predictive models more interpretable and transparent. Automated machine learning (AutoML) is simplifying the process of building predictive models, making them accessible to a broader audience.

Our data-driven environment has made predictive analytics an essential tool. Its ability to anticipate future outcomes based on data empowers organizations to make more informed decisions, reduce risks, and seize opportunities. Predictive analytics will continue to develop as data becomes more readily available and technology progresses, influencing a future in which success will mostly depend on having the foresight and making data-driven decisions. It is a testament to the transformative power of data science and its capacity to illuminate the path forward.

Prescriptive Analytics

Prescriptive analytics represents the pinnacle of data science, going beyond predicting future outcomes to recommending the best course of action. It permits organizations to make data-driven decisions by optimizing choices and actions based on historical data, predictive models, and business rules. In this section, we delve into the significance of prescriptive analytics, its methodologies, and the transformative impact it has across industries, enabling smarter, more efficient, and proactive decision-making.

Prescriptive analytics takes the insights acquired from descriptive and predictive analytics a step further by recommending the best actions to achieve desired outcomes. It combines data-driven predictions with optimization techniques, ensuring that decisions are not just informed but also strategically optimal. Essentially, it guides organizations on what actions to take to maximize their objectives.

Prescriptive analytics employs a variety of methodologies to generate recommendations. Linear and integer programming, for instance, help optimize resource allocation and scheduling problems. Decision trees and decision analysis are used to assess different decision paths and their respective outcomes. Simulation modeling enables organizations to test various scenarios and evaluate their impacts.

Machine learning is also vital in prescriptive analytics. Reinforcement learning, for example, is used to optimize decision-making processes in dynamic environments. Deep reinforcement learning techniques, with their ability to handle complex and high-dimensional data, are applied to tasks such as autonomous vehicle control and game strategy optimization.

Prescriptive analytics finds applications across a wide range of industries. In supply chain management, it helps optimize inventory levels, distribution routes, and production schedules, reducing costs and enhancing customer satisfaction. In healthcare, prescriptive analytics assists in treatment planning and resource allocation, guaranteeing that patients receive the most effective care. In finance, it optimizes investment portfolios and risk management strategies, maximizing returns while minimizing exposure.

Prescriptive analytics is a cornerstone of modern business intelligence (BI) and decision support systems. Organizations employ BI platforms to integrate prescriptive models into their decision-making processes. These platforms provide decision-makers with actionable insights, highlighting the optimal actions to take based on the current context and objectives.

Prescriptive analytics is not without its challenges. It relies heavily on accurate and up-to-date data, making data quality a paramount concern. Ethical considerations, such as fairness and transparency, must be addressed to ensure that recommendations do not perpetuate biases or discriminate against certain groups. The complexity of optimization algorithms can pose computational challenges, demanding specialized tools and high-performance computing resources.

The future of prescriptive analytics holds exciting possibilities. As computing power and data availability grow, prescriptive models will become increasingly advanced and capable of handling vast and complex decision spaces. Explainable AI (XAI) will play a crucial role in making prescriptive models more interpretable and transparent, fostering trust in their recommendations. Automated prescriptive analytics tools will become more accessible, enabling organizations of all sizes to leverage their power.

Prescriptive analytics represents a transformative force in our data-driven world. It goes beyond informing decisions; it guides organizations on the most strategic actions to take, ensuring that resources are allocated optimally and objectives are met efficiently. As technology advances and data continues to proliferate, prescriptive analytics will continue to evolve, shaping a future where data-driven decision-making is not just predictive but also prescriptive, enabling organizations to thrive in an increasingly complex and dynamic world. It is a testament to the potential of data science to empower informed and strategic decision-making.

Case Studies on Successful Insights

Data-driven decision-making has become a fundamental driver of success across industries, enabling organizations to uncover valuable insights, enhance efficiency, and drive innovation. In this section, we explore several case studies that illustrate the transformative impact of data- driven insights in diverse domains, ranging from e- commerce to healthcare and beyond. These real-world examples demonstrate how data, when harnessed effectively, can empower organizations to make informed choices that lead to substantial improvements and competitive advantages.

A large percentage of purchases at the famous e-commerce giant Amazon are generated by its personalized recommendation system. By analyzing users' browsing and purchase history, as well as the behavior of similar customers, Amazon's algorithms generate product recommendations tailored to individual preferences. This data-driven approach has not only increased customer satisfaction but also boosted revenue. Studies have shown that Amazon's recommendation engine can account for up to 35% of its total sales, exemplifying the immense impact of data-driven insights in the e-commerce sector.

Netflix, the streaming entertainment powerhouse, relies heavily on data-driven insights to enhance user engagement and retention. Its recommendation system assesses users' viewing history, ratings, and interactions with the platform to suggest content tailored to their tastes. Statistics show that suggestions impact almost 80% of the content viewed on Netflix, which is one reason why this personalized strategy has been crucial to the company's success. By leveraging data to guide content recommendations, Netflix keeps subscribers engaged and invested in its service.

Google Maps exemplifies the power of data-driven insights in optimizing real-time decision-making. The app uses historical traffic data, user location information, and real-time traffic updates to provide users with accurate travel time estimates and route recommendations. This data-driven approach not only aids commuters in avoiding traffic congestion but also enables Google to collect valuable data on traffic patterns. The insights derived from this data are then used to improve navigation algorithms and enhance the accuracy of predictions, benefiting millions of users worldwide.

IBM's Watson, a powerful AI platform, has made significant inroads into the healthcare sector. Watson for Oncology, for instance, analyzes vast amounts of medical literature, patient records, and clinical guidelines to assist oncologists in formulating personalized treatment plans for cancer patients. By providing data-driven insights, Watson helps clinicians make informed decisions about treatment options, ultimately enhancing patient outcomes. Case studies have demonstrated that Watson's recommendations align with expert oncologists' decisions in approximately 96% of breast cancer cases, showcasing the potential of data-driven insights to revolutionize healthcare.

Procter & Gamble (P&G), a consumer goods conglomerate, has embraced data-driven insights to optimize its supply chain and inventory management. By integrating data from various sources, including sales data, production schedules, and weather forecasts, P&G can anticipate fluctuations in demand and adjust its inventory levels accordingly. This data-driven approach has not only reduced excess inventory but also ensured product availability on store shelves. P&G's success story demonstrates how data-driven insights can drive cost savings and operational efficiency.

Airbnb, a platform for short-term vacation rentals, employs data-driven insights to implement dynamic pricing strategies. By analyzing factors such as location, property type, time of booking, and local events, Airbnb's algorithms adjust rental prices in real-time to match supply and demand. This data-driven approach has enabled hosts to maximize their earnings while ensuring competitive prices for guests. Case studies have indicated that hosts who use Airbnb's dynamic pricing feature can increase their revenue by up to 40%, underscoring the potential of data-driven insights to optimize pricing strategies.

Tesla, the electric vehicle manufacturer, utilizes data-driven insights to enhance its Autopilot feature. Tesla vehicles are equipped with sensors and cameras that collect data on road conditions, traffic, and driver behavior. This data is then used to improve and fine-tune the Autopilot's capabilities through over-the-air updates. Tesla's iterative approach to data-driven development has led to significant improvements in the performance and safety of its Autopilot system, exemplifying how data can drive continuous innovation in the automotive industry.

The case studies presented here serve as compelling examples of how data-driven insights are transforming businesses and industries across the globe. Whether it's personalized recommendations in e-commerce, optimized healthcare treatments, or dynamic pricing strategies, data-driven decision-making is a fundamental driver of success. These real-world examples illustrate the immense potential of data-driven insights to enhance efficiency, drive innovation, and empower organizations to make informed choices that lead to substantial improvements and competitive advantages. In an increasingly data-centric world, the ability to harness the power of data-driven insights is a defining factor in achieving success and remaining at the forefront of innovation.

CHAPTER IX

Implementing Data Science Projects

Building a Data Science Team

In today's data-driven world, organizations are recognizing the pivotal role of data science in extracting insights, making knowledgeable decisions, and gaining a competitive edge. To harness the power of data, building a skilled and cohesive data science team is essential. In this section, we explore the process of constructing a successful data science team, from defining roles and skills to fostering a collaborative culture and staying abreast of evolving trends in this dynamic field.

The first step in building an effective data science team is defining clear roles and responsibilities. Data science encompasses a broad spectrum of tasks, including data collection, cleaning, analysis, machine learning, and data engineering. Therefore, it's crucial to delineate roles such as data scientists, data engineers, machine learning engineers, and data analysts. Each role should have well-defined responsibilities to ensure that the team operates cohesively.

Once roles are defined, it's vital to identify the skills and expertise necessary for each role. Data scientists should possess strong statistical and analytical skills, in addition to expertise in programming languages such as R or Python. Data engineers should excel in data architecture and database management, while machine learning engineers need expertise in building and deploying machine learning models. Collaboratively, the team should have a comprehensive understanding of data pipelines, cloud computing, and domain-specific knowledge relevant to the organization's industry.

Recruiting top talent is the cornerstone of building a successful data science team. The demand for skilled data professionals is high, and competition for talent is fierce. To attract the best candidates, organizations should offer competitive compensation packages, emphasize their commitment to data-driven decision-making, and provide opportunities for professional growth and development. Additionally, creating a diverse and inclusive hiring process can help foster a team with a wide range of perspectives and experiences.

Collaboration is essential for a data science team to thrive. Encouraging an environment where team members openly share ideas, insights, and challenges is crucial. Regular meetings, cross-functional collaboration with other departments, and knowledge-sharing sessions can help foster a culture of teamwork and innovation. Effective communication and teamwork are key to translating data insights into actionable strategies.

The field of data science is constantly evolving, with new techniques, tools, and technologies emerging regularly. It's imperative for organizations to invest in continuous learning for their data science teams. Encourage team members to stay updated on the latest developments by attending conferences, workshops, and online courses. Supporting certification programs can also help team members acquire specialized skills.

Data scientists rely heavily on access to high-quality data and advanced technology. Organizations must ensure that their data science team has access to a robust data infrastructure, including data warehouses and data lakes. Cloud computing platforms like AWS, Azure, or Google Cloud can provide the necessary infrastructure for data storage and processing. Access to cutting-edge tools and software is equally important, as it enables the team to conduct advanced analyses and build machine learning models effectively.

Ethical considerations are paramount in data science, especially when handling sensitive data. Organizations should establish ethical guidelines and best practices for their data science team, ensuring that data privacy and security are upheld. Encourage team members to follow ethical principles, such as transparency, fairness, and accountability, in their work. Additionally, staying compliant with data protection regulations, such as GDPR or CCPA, is essential to maintain trust and avoid legal issues.

Measuring the performance of a data science team is essential to track progress and make necessary improvements. Define key performance indicators (KPIs) and metrics that align with the organization's goals. These may include the accuracy of predictive models, the speed of data processing, or the impact of data-driven insights on business outcomes. Regularly evaluate team performance and provide feedback to help team members grow and excel in their roles.

The data science field is marked by rapid change and innovation. Organizations and their data science teams must remain agile and adaptable. Embrace iterative development and agile methodologies to respond quickly to evolving business needs. Encourage experimentation and a willingness to explore new approaches and technologies. By staying agile, the team can remain at the forefront of data science advancements.

Ultimately, the success of a data science team depends on the organization's commitment to a data-driven culture. Leadership should lead by example, making data-informed decisions and emphasizing the importance of data across the organization. Ensure that data science insights are integrated into the decision-making process, and highlight success stories that showcase the impact of data-driven initiatives.

Building a data science team is a multifaceted endeavor that requires careful planning, recruitment, and a commitment to continuous improvement. A well-structured and collaborative team can unlock the full potential of data, driving innovation, improving decision-making, and delivering tangible results for the organization. By defining roles, nurturing talent, fostering a collaborative culture, and staying adaptable, organizations can navigate the path to data-driven success and embrace a future powered by data.

Project Management in Data Science

The field of data science has emerged as a transformative force, empowering organizations to extract insights from vast and complex datasets. Yet, harnessing the power of data science effectively requires more than just technical expertise. It demands meticulous project management to navigate the multifaceted challenges, align with organizational goals, and ensure that data-driven insights translate into real-world impact. In this section, we delve into the intricacies of project management in data science, exploring its essential principles, methodologies, and best practices.

Data science projects differ significantly from traditional IT or software development initiatives. They are inherently iterative and exploratory, often dealing with messy, unstructured data. The high degree of uncertainty and the need for continuous adaptation make data science projects prone to scope changes and challenges in defining clear project objectives.

Data science projects typically follow a lifecycle that includes data collection, data cleaning and preprocessing, exploratory data analysis, modeling, evaluation, and deployment. Effective project management involves overseeing each phase, ensuring data quality, and maintaining a clear focus on the project's goals.

A successful data science project relies on a multidisciplinary team, including data scientists, data engineers, domain experts, and project managers. The team's diversity ensures a holistic approach, with domain experts providing crucial context and data scientists leveraging their analytical skills.

One of the important aspects of project management in data science is defining the problem accurately. A well-defined problem statement not only guides the project but also determines the success criteria. Project managers must collaborate closely with stakeholders to ensure that expectations are aligned and the project's goals are clearly articulated.

Agile methodologies, like Scrum and Kanban, are well-suited for data science projects. They promote flexibility, adaptability, and frequent collaboration between team members and stakeholders. Agile practices, like regular stand-up meetings and sprint planning, help keep projects on track and responsive to changing requirements.

Data governance ensures that data is handled responsibly, respecting privacy regulations and ethical considerations. Project managers play a vital role in establishing data governance practices, including data anonymization, encryption, and access control. Ethical considerations, such as bias mitigation and fairness, must also be integrated into project planning and execution.

Data science projects often involve experimentation and prototyping. Project managers should foster a culture of experimentation, where failure is seen as an opportunity for learning. Prototypes can help stakeholders visualize the potential impact of data-driven solutions.

Effective project management includes thorough documentation of project decisions, data sources, methodologies, and results. Clear and regular communication with stakeholders is essential to make sure that everyone is informed about project progress, challenges, and outcomes.

Project managers must oversee the rigorous evaluation of machine learning models. This includes cross-validation, testing against holdout datasets, and performance metrics that align with project objectives. Model validation ensures that the insights generated are reliable and accurate.

Translating data-driven insights into action requires a well-executed deployment phase. Project managers must collaborate with IT teams to ensure a smooth deployment process. Post-deployment, continuous monitoring and feedback mechanisms help maintain the effectiveness of the solution and make necessary adjustments over time.

Scalability is a crucial consideration for data science projects. As the project matures, it may need to handle larger datasets or increased user loads. Project managers should plan for scalability and ensure that long-term maintenance is sustainable.

Quantifying the Return on Investment (ROI) of a data science project is often challenging but essential. Project managers must work with stakeholders to define measurable success criteria and track them throughout the project's lifecycle. This allows organizations to assess the value generated by data science initiatives.

Every data science project presents opportunities for learning and improvement. After project completion, project managers should conduct post-mortem assessments to identify successes and areas for enhancement. This knowledge can inform future projects and contribute to organizational growth.

In an era driven by data, effective project management is the linchpin that ensures data science initiatives align with organizational objectives, navigate complexities, and maximize impact. It demands a combination of technical expertise, agile methodologies, ethical considerations, and clear communication. The role of the project manager plays a pivotal role in orchestrating the diverse talents of data scientists, engineers, and domain experts, and guiding them toward meaningful results. As organizations invest in data science to gain competitive advantages and drive innovation, the importance of skilled project managers in this dynamic field cannot be overstated. They are the navigators, steering data science projects toward success and enabling data-driven transformation in the modern world.

Challenges in Implementation

Data science projects hold immense promise for organizations seeking to leverage data for insights, automation, and strategic decision-making. However, the journey from project inception to successful implementation is riddled with challenges. In this section, we explore the multifaceted obstacles that organizations encounter when implementing data science projects, from data quality and talent shortages to ethical considerations and organizational alignment. Understanding and addressing these challenges is pivotal in realizing the full potential of data science initiatives.

Data is the lifeblood of data science, and its quality and availability are foundational to project success. Data can be messy, incomplete, and inconsistent, which can hinder the development of accurate models and insights. Organizations often face challenges in acquiring and preparing data for analysis. Data quality issues can arise from disparate data sources, outdated information, or inadequate data governance practices. Data cleaning, preprocessing, and integration become critical steps in the project implementation process, consuming a significant amount of time and resources.

The shortage of skilled data professionals is a pervasive challenge in the implementation of data science projects. Data scientists, data engineers, as well as machine learning specialists are in high demand, leading to fierce competition for talent. Organizations may struggle to find individuals with the right skill set and experience to execute complex data science initiatives. Furthermore, retaining top talent in a competitive job market can be equally challenging. Bridging the talent gap requires strategic recruitment, training, and upskilling efforts.

As data science projects evolve, scalability and infrastructure become prominent concerns. Handling large datasets and complex algorithms demands robust computing infrastructure. Organizations often find themselves grappling with decisions related to on-premises versus cloud-based solutions. Scaling up infrastructure to meet growing computational demands while optimizing costs is a delicate balancing act. Failure to address scalability issues can lead to bottlenecks and project delays.

Data science projects are not immune to ethical dilemmas. The use of sensitive data, algorithmic bias, and the potential for privacy infringements necessitate a careful and ethical approach. Organizations must grapple with questions about consent, transparency, and fairness. Ethical concerns can pose a significant challenge in project implementation, requiring organizations to establish clear ethical guidelines, governance frameworks, and mechanisms for ongoing ethical review.

Data science projects often require cross-functional collaboration and alignment within the organization. Achieving buy-in from different departments and stakeholders can be challenging, as not everyone may fully comprehend the potential benefits of data science. Resistance to change, organizational silos, and conflicting priorities can hinder project progress. Effective communication, education, and a shared vision for data- driven decision-making are crucial for overcoming these challenges.

The "black-box" nature of some machine learning models presents challenges in project implementation, particularly when decision-makers require transparency and interpretability. Ensuring that models can be understood and their predictions explained is essential, especially in industries with regulatory requirements or when human decisions are involved. Balancing model complexity with interpretability can be a delicate task, often requiring trade-offs.

Data science projects can be lengthy and resource-intensive endeavors. Effective project management is vital in ensuring that projects stay on track and within budget. Organizations may encounter difficulties in accurately estimating project timelines, managing scope creep, and aligning project schedules with business objectives. Balancing the need for a profound analysis with timely results can be challenging.

Data security and privacy concerns are paramount, especially when handling sensitive or personal information. Privacy violations and data breaches can have serious legal and reputational consequences. Organizations must invest in robust data security measures, implement data protection protocols, and comply with relevant regulations, such as GDPR or CCPA. Ensuring data security and privacy can be resource-intensive but is non-negotiable.

Creating a machine learning model is just the beginning; deploying and maintaining it in a real-world environment can be challenging. Ensuring that models remain accurate and up-to-date requires continuous monitoring and retraining. Organizations may encounter difficulties in integrating models into existing systems, managing model versioning, and ensuring that predictions align with business objectives. The long-term sustainability of models is a crucial aspect of project implementation.

Demonstrating the value and return on investment (ROI) of data science projects can be challenging, particularly in the absence of clear benchmarks and metrics. Calculating the impact of data-driven insights on business outcomes can be complex. Organizations must devise mechanisms to measure the success of data science initiatives, align them with strategic goals, and communicate their value to stakeholders effectively.

The implementation of data science projects is a complex and multifaceted process, fraught with challenges. Organizations that navigate these challenges successfully can unlock the transformative potential of data science, driving innovation, efficiency, and informed decision-making. Addressing data quality, talent shortages, scalability, ethical considerations, organizational alignment, interpretability, project management, data security, model deployment, and ROI requires a holistic and strategic approach. By recognizing these challenges and investing in the necessary resources and expertise, organizations can harness the power of data science to thrive in an increasingly data-driven world. It is a journey that demands resilience, adaptability, and a commitment to data-driven excellence.

Measuring Success

Data science has become an indispensable tool for organizations across various industries, promising to unlock valuable insights, optimize operations, and drive strategic decision-making. However, measuring the success of data science projects is a nuanced and multifaceted endeavor. In this section, we delve into the intricacies of evaluating the impact and effectiveness of data science initiatives, from defining success metrics to considering ethical considerations and demonstrating value to stakeholders.

To calculate the success of data science projects, organizations must first define clear and relevant success metrics. These metrics should align with the project's goals and objectives, which could vary widely depending on the project's purpose. For example, in a predictive maintenance project for manufacturing, success may be measured by the reduction in equipment downtime and maintenance costs. In a marketing campaign optimization project, success might be gauged by improvements in customer engagement, conversion rates, or return on investment (ROI).

Accuracy and performance metrics are often central to assessing the success of data science models. For predictive models, metrics such as accuracy, precision, recall, F1-score, and ROC AUC (Receiver Operating Characteristic Area Under the Curve) are commonly used to evaluate model performance. In regression tasks, metrics like mean squared error (MSE) or root mean squared error (RMSE) quantify the model's predictive accuracy. It's essential to select the appropriate metrics based on the specific problem and the business impact of prediction errors.

Ultimately, the success of a data science project should be measured by its impact on the organization's bottom line and strategic objectives. Calculating the return on investment (ROI) is a vital component of measuring success. ROI quantifies the value generated by the project relative to its costs. It considers both tangible benefits, such as increased revenue or cost savings, and intangible benefits, like improved customer satisfaction or brand reputation. Demonstrating a positive ROI is a compelling way to showcase the project's success to stakeholders.

Measuring the success of data science projects also involves ethical considerations. Ethical metrics should address issues related to fairness, transparency, and data privacy. For instance, assessing algorithmic bias and ensuring that predictions are fair across different demographic groups is crucial, especially in applications like lending or hiring. Additionally, evaluating the model's transparency and the extent to which it provides interpretable results can be essential, particularly in highly regulated industries.

The satisfaction of key stakeholders is an essential aspect of project success. Conducting surveys or obtaining feedback from end-users and decision-makers can provide insights into the project's usability and perceived value. High levels of stakeholder satisfaction often correlate with successful project implementation. Additionally, tracking the adoption rate of data-driven insights and tools within the organization can be a valuable success metric. A high adoption rate indicates that the project's results are integrated into daily operations and decision-making processes.

The success of data science projects is not limited to their initial outcomes but extends to their ongoing performance and adaptability. Monitoring the model's performance over time, especially in dynamic environments, ensures that it continues to provide accurate and valuable predictions. Regular model retraining and updates, as well as the ability to adapt to changing data and business conditions, contribute to sustained success.

Effectively communicating the value generated by data science projects is a critical step in measuring success. Stakeholders, including executives, investors, and end-users, may not possess a deep understanding of the technical intricacies of data science. Therefore, it is incumbent upon data scientists and project managers to present results in a clear and compelling manner. Visualizations, reports, and presentations that highlight the project's impact on key performance indicators (KPIs) can help stakeholders appreciate the value delivered.

Successful data science projects are often part of a broader data-driven strategy. As such, they contribute to an organization's continuous improvement efforts. Measuring success should include an element of iterative learning, where insights from one project inform subsequent projects. Organizations should establish mechanisms for capturing lessons learned, best practices, and opportunities for further optimization. This approach ensures that data science projects contribute not only to immediate goals but also to the organization's long-term data maturity and competitiveness.

Measuring the success of data science projects transcends traditional metrics and accuracy evaluations. It encompasses a holistic view of impact, aligning project goals with business objectives, considering ethical considerations, and demonstrating value to stakeholders. Success metrics should reflect not only the technical aspects of model performance but also the real-world consequences of data-driven insights. By defining success metrics thoughtfully, considering ethical implications, and effectively communicating value, organizations can harness the full potential of data science to drive innovation, efficiency, and data-driven decision-making. Ultimately, the success of data science projects is not solely about the numbers; it's about the tangible and lasting impact they have on organizations and the broader society they serve.

CHAPTER X

Future Trends in Data Science

Emerging Technologies in Data Science

Data science is a dynamic field, constantly evolving to meet the ever-growing demands for harnessing data to drive innovation and make informed decisions. Emerging technologies play a pivotal role in shaping the future of data science, offering new avenues for data collection, analysis, and application. In this section, we explore some of the most promising emerging technologies in data science, from AI and machine learning advancements to edge computing and quantum computing, and their potential to revolutionize industries and enhance our understanding of the data-driven world.

Artificial Intelligence and also Machine Learning have already made significant strides in data science, but they continue to evolve rapidly. Advancements in deep learning, reinforcement learning, and natural language processing are enabling machines to perform increasingly complex tasks, like image recognition, language translation, and autonomous decision-making. These technologies are driving breakthroughs in fields like healthcare, finance, and autonomous systems. In healthcare, AI-powered diagnostic tools are improving disease detection, while in finance, algorithmic trading strategies are becoming more sophisticated. The ability of AI and ML to process massive datasets and identify patterns that humans might overlook holds tremendous potential for unlocking valuable insights.

Edge computing is reshaping how data is processed and analyzed by bringing computation closer to the data source. Instead of sending all data to centralized cloud servers, edge devices, such as IoT sensors or edge servers, process data locally. This reduces latency, enhances real-time decision-making, and conserves bandwidth. In applications such as industrial automation and driverless cars, edge computing is critical for processing data quickly and efficiently. It also addresses privacy and security concerns by minimizing data transfer to centralized locations, making it a game-changer in data science.

A paradigm shift in computational power can be seen in quantum computing. Quantum computers is still in its infancy, yet it has the ability to tackle complicated problems exponentially quicker than classical computers. In data science, quantum computing could revolutionize optimization problems, cryptography, and simulations. For example, it could dramatically speed up the training of machine learning models, enabling the analysis of massive datasets that were previously impractical. While commercial quantum computers are in their early stages, they hold immense promise for the future of data science.

Blockchain, initially associated with cryptocurrencies like Bitcoin, has found applications beyond finance. Its decentralized and immutable ledger technology can enhance data security, transparency, and trust in various industries. In data science, blockchain can be used to secure and verify data, ensuring its integrity and origin. This is particularly valuable in fields such as supply chain management, where tracking the provenance of products is crucial, or in healthcare, where patient data security is paramount. Blockchain's potential for enabling secure data sharing and reducing fraud is increasingly recognized.

Automated Machine Learning (AutoML) is democratizing machine learning by automating many of the complex and time-consuming tasks involved in model development. It simplifies the process of feature engineering, model selection, and hyperparameter tuning, making machine learning more accessible to non-experts. AutoML platforms like Google's AutoML, Microsoft's Azure AutoML, and H2O.ai's Driverless AI are gaining popularity. They allow organizations to leverage machine learning without extensive data science expertise, accelerating the deployment of predictive models across various industries.

As AI systems become more intricate, there is a growing requirement for transparency and interpretability. Explainable AI (XAI) focuses on making AI models more understandable and explainable to humans. This technology is crucial in applications where decisions have major consequences, like healthcare and finance. XAI techniques provide insights into how models arrive at their decisions, helping to build trust and ensure accountability. It's an essential advancement for bridging the gap between machine learning and human decision-makers.

Generating synthetic data has gained attention as a way to overcome privacy concerns and data scarcity issues. Synthetic data is artificially created data that retains statistical properties of real data but doesn't contain sensitive information. It can be utilized for training machine learning models and conducting data science experiments without exposing sensitive information. This technology is particularly relevant in healthcare and finance, where privacy regulations are stringent, and access to real data is limited.

Augmented Reality (or AR) and Virtual Reality (or VR) technologies are expanding the possibilities of data visualization and exploration. In data science, they enable users to interact with complex datasets in immersive environments, providing a deeper understanding of data patterns and trends. AR and VR are increasingly used for data analytics, enhancing the ability to explore 3D data visualizations, conduct simulations, and collaborate in virtual spaces. These technologies offer a new dimension to data-driven decision-making.

Natural Language Processing (NLP) continues to advance, driven by deep learning techniques and increased computational power. Models like GPT-3 and BERT have demonstrated remarkable language understanding capabilities. This technology is transforming customer service with chatbots and virtual assistants, making them more conversational and capable of understanding context. In data science, NLP is used for sentiment analysis, text classification, and automated content generation, among other applications.

As data science becomes more pervasive, addressing ethical concerns and mitigating biases in data and algorithms is crucial. Emerging technologies include tools for bias detection and mitigation, fairness-aware machine learning, and ethical AI frameworks. These tools help organizations ensure that their data science projects adhere to ethical principles, promote fairness, and avoid unintended consequences.

Emerging technologies are propelling data science into an era of unprecedented possibilities. AI and ML advancements, edge computing, quantum computing, blockchain, AutoML, XAI, synthetic data generation, AR, VR, NLP, and ethics tools are transforming how we collect, analyze, and apply data. These technologies have the ability to fully transform various industries, including manufacturing, transportation, healthcare, and finance.

As data science continues to evolve, its ability to drive innovation and make data-driven decisions is becoming increasingly accessible, powerful, and transformative.

The future of data science is indeed an exciting journey into the unknown, where technology and data intersect to unlock new frontiers of knowledge and insight.

AI and Machine Learning Advancements

Artificial Intelligence (or AI) and Machine Learning (or ML) have evolved exponentially in recent years, ushering in a transformative era across industries. These advancements have redefined what is possible in data analysis, automation, and decision-making. In this section, we explore the latest breakthroughs in AI and ML, from deep learning and reinforcement learning to natural language processing and computer vision. These technological strides are reshaping businesses, healthcare, education, and more, unlocking new opportunities and addressing complex challenges.

A subset of machine learning that has emerged as a driving force behind many AI advancements is known as deep learning. This approach involves neural networks with multiple layers (deep neural networks) that can automatically discover intricate patterns and representations from data. Convolutional Neural Networks (CNNs) excel in image recognition tasks, while Recurrent Neural Networks (RNNs) are proficient in sequential data analysis. Transformers, a relatively recent architectural innovation, have revolutionized natural language processing tasks. The ability to process vast datasets and automatically learn hierarchical features has led to breakthroughs in computer vision, speech recognition, and language understanding.

Reinforcement learning (RL) has gained prominence in AI as a result of its success in training agents to make sequential decisions in dynamic environments. RL algorithms use trial-and-error to learn optimal strategies by interacting with an environment and acquiring rewards or penalties for actions taken. Notable achievements include DeepMind's AlphaGo, which defeated world champion Go players, and RL applications in robotics, where autonomous systems learn to perform tasks through interaction with the physical world. RL is poised to revolutionize fields like autonomous driving, game design, and healthcare treatment optimization.

Transfer learning and pre-trained models have democratized AI development by enabling practitioners to leverage models trained on vast datasets. Pre-trained models like OpenAI's GPT (Generative Pre-trained Transformer) and BERT (Bidirectional Encoder Representations from Transformers) have demonstrated astounding capabilities in natural language understanding and generation. Researchers and developers can fine-tune these models for specific tasks, reducing the need for massive labeled datasets and significantly speeding up model development. This approach has unlocked applications in sentiment analysis, language translation, and chatbot development.

Generative Adversarial Networks (GANs) have revolutionized the generation of synthetic data and creative content. A generator and a discriminator are two neural networks that compete with one another to form a GAN. The generator produces data, such as images or text, and the discriminator evaluates its authenticity. This adversarial process results in the generation of high-quality, realistic data. GANs have applications in image synthesis, art generation, data augmentation, and deepfake detection. They hold potential for revolutionizing content creation, design, and data augmentation in machine learning.

It is now more important than ever for AI systems to be transparent and comprehensible. Explainable AI (XAI) focuses on making AI models more understandable and explainable to humans. Techniques like LIME (Local Interpretable Model-agnostic Explanations) and SHAP

(SHapley Additive exPlanations) provide insights into how models arrive at their decisions. This is crucial in applications where decisions have significant consequences, such as healthcare diagnostics or financial risk assessment. XAI fosters trust, accountability, and ethical AI deployment.

Federated learning addresses data privacy concerns while advancing machine learning capabilities. It enables training machine learning models across decentralized devices or servers while keeping data localized and secure. This approach has applications in healthcare (e.g., analyzing patient data from various hospitals without centralized data sharing) and edge computing (e.g., training models on IoT devices). Federated learning aligns with privacy regulations like GDPR and CCPA, making it a promising avenue for privacy-conscious industries.

Automated Machine Learning (AutoML) platforms automate many aspects of machine learning model development, making AI more accessible to non-experts. These platforms handle tasks such as feature engineering, model selection, and hyperparameter tuning. Cloud providers like Google, Microsoft, and Amazon offer AutoML services that streamline the machine learning pipeline. AutoML democratizes AI by reducing the technical barriers to entry, allowing organizations to harness machine learning without extensive data science expertise.

Edge AI brings AI capabilities directly to devices, bypassing the need for constant cloud connectivity. This is especially crucial in applications requiring real-time decision-making, like autonomous vehicles and IoT sensors. Edge AI devices, equipped with specialized hardware accelerators, can process data locally, reducing latency and conserving bandwidth. Edge AI enhances security, privacy, and reliability by minimizing data transfer to centralized servers.

Quantum machine learning combines quantum computing with machine learning to solve complex problems exponentially faster than classical computers. While still in the experimental stage, quantum machine learning holds immense promise. It could revolutionize fields like materials science, cryptography, drug discovery, and optimization problems. Quantum algorithms, such as Grover's search and Shor's factoring, promise to disrupt existing computational paradigms.

AI advancements are making significant contributions to healthcare. Machine learning models can analyze medical images (e.g., X-rays and MRIs) for disease detection, assist in drug discovery, predict patient outcomes, and even optimize treatment plans. AI-powered chatbots and virtual assistants are improving patient engagement and telemedicine services. In the fight against diseases like COVID-19, AI models have aided in epidemiological predictions and vaccine development.

The ever-accelerating advancements in AI and machine learning are expanding the possibilities of what can be achieved with data-driven technology. Deep learning, reinforcement learning, transfer learning, GANs, XAI, federated learning, AutoML, edge AI, quantum machine learning, and AI applications in healthcare are redefining industries and addressing complex problems. The democratization of AI, coupled with its increasing interpretability and privacy-aware approaches, is paving the way for AI adoption across diverse domains. As these technologies evolve, they hold the potential to revolutionize our understanding of data, drive innovation, and shape the future in ways we have yet to fully envision. The landscape of AI and machine learning is one of perpetual transformation, and it promises to leave an indelible mark on our world.

Ethical AI and Responsible Data Science

In an era defined by the rapid advancement of artificial intelligence (AI) and data science, the ethical dimensions of these technologies have taken center stage. As AI systems make consequential decisions, and data science delves deeper into our personal and societal data, questions of ethics, fairness, transparency, and accountability become paramount. In this section, we explore the concept of ethical AI and responsible data science, examining the ethical challenges that arise and the strategies and frameworks in place to ensure that these technologies serve the betterment of humanity while respecting individual rights, privacy, and societal values.

The advent of AI has brought with it a host of ethical dilemmas. AI algorithms can inadvertently preserve biases present in training data, leading to unfair or discriminatory outcomes. For instance, AI-driven hiring tools may inadvertently favor one demographic group over others, perpetuating historical inequalities. Ethical considerations also extend to the use of AI in decision-making processes in critical domains like criminal justice, healthcare, and finance, where AI systems can have profound real-world impacts on individuals' lives.

To address the challenges of fairness and bias in AI, researchers and practitioners are developing methods and frameworks that promote equitable outcomes. Fairness-aware machine learning techniques aim to identify and mitigate biases in training data and algorithms. Techniques such as reweighting, adversarial training, and disparate impact analysis help create AI models that provide equitable outcomes across different demographic groups. The adoption of fairness-aware practices is vital for building AI systems that respect human values and promote equal opportunities.

AI systems often operate as "black boxes," making it difficult to comprehend how they arrive at their decisions. This lack of transparency can erode trust and accountability. The field of explainable AI (or XAI) aims to make AI systems more transparent and interpretable to humans. Techniques like feature attribution, rule-based explanations, and model-agnostic methods shed light on the decision-making processes of AI models. This not only enhances trust but also helps identify and rectify biased or unethical decisions.

Responsible data science requires robust data privacy and security measures to protect individuals' sensitive information. The misuse or mishandling of personal data can result in privacy breaches, identity theft, and other forms of harm. Regulations like the GDPR and the CCPA establish guidelines for data handling and user consent. Organizations must adhere to these regulations, implement data anonymization and encryption techniques, and adopt strong data governance practices to safeguard data privacy and security.

Obtaining informed permission from individuals for data collection and processing is a fundamental ethical principle. Users should have a clear understanding of how their data will be used and the potential consequences. Consent mechanisms should be transparent, accessible, and provide users with meaningful choices. Ethical data science involves respecting user preferences and allowing individuals to exercise control over their data.

Accountability is a critical aspect of responsible AI and data science. Organizations that deploy AI systems must take responsibility for their actions and outcomes. Algorithmic auditing, similar to financial audits, involves assessing AI systems for fairness, bias, and ethical considerations. Independent audits can help identify and rectify issues in AI systems, ensuring that they meet their ethical standards and societal values.

Ethical frameworks, such as IEEE Global Initiative on Ethics of Autonomous and Intelligent Systems and also the Principles for AI, provide guidance for developing, deploying, and regulating AI technologies responsibly. These frameworks emphasize values like transparency, fairness, accountability, and privacy. By adhering to ethical guidelines, organizations can ensure that their AI and data science initiatives align with broader ethical principles.

Ethical considerations in AI and data science are not one-size-fits-all. Cultural and global variations play a significant role in shaping ethical norms and practices. What is considered ethical in one culture may differ from another. Organizations operating in diverse regions must navigate these nuances and adapt their AI and data science practices to align with local ethical standards.

Natural Language Processing (NLP) is an area where ethical concerns regarding bias are particularly pertinent. Language models trained on large corpora of text can inherit biases present in the data. Researchers are actively working on debiasing techniques for NLP models to ensure that they produce fair and unbiased language generation. This is especially important in applications like chatbots, virtual assistants, and automated content generation.

As autonomous systems, such as self-driving cars and drones, become more prevalent, ethical considerations come to the forefront. These systems make decisions that can impact human safety and well-being. Ethical frameworks for autonomous systems include principles like minimizing harm, ensuring transparency in decision-making, and establishing fallback mechanisms in cases of unforeseen circumstances.

Ethical AI and responsible data science are indispensable in ensuring that technology serves the betterment of society without causing harm or perpetuating bias. The challenges are multifaceted, ranging from bias mitigation to transparency, data privacy, and cultural considerations. However, by adopting ethical frameworks, implementing fairness-aware practices, and prioritizing transparency and accountability, organizations and researchers can strike a balance between innovation and ethics. Ultimately, the ethical foundations of AI and data science are not constraints but guiding principles that contribute to technology that respects human values and promotes the common good. The path to responsible technology is an ongoing journey, where ethical considerations evolve in parallel with technological advancements.'

The Future Landscape of Data Science

The field of data science has undergone a remarkable evolution in recent years, becoming an indispensable tool for organizations and industries across the globe. However, the journey is far from over. As we look to the future, the landscape of data science is poised for further transformation, driven by technological advancements, expanding applications, and evolving challenges. In this section, we explore the key trends and developments that will transform the future of data science, from the rise of AI and automation to the ethical considerations that must accompany this progress.

One of the most significant trends shaping the future of data science is the integration of artificial intelligence (AI) and automation. AI-powered tools and algorithms are increasingly automating tasks that were once labor-intensive, such as data cleaning, preprocessing, and even model selection. Automated machine learning (AutoML) platforms are making it easier for non-experts to build and deploy machine learning models, democratizing data science and accelerating the development of AI applications.

As the impact of data science grows, so too do the ethical considerations surrounding it. The future of data science will see a heightened focus on ethical and responsible practices. This includes addressing issues related to bias, fairness, transparency, and data privacy. Ethical frameworks and guidelines will play a crucial role in ensuring that data science serves the betterment of society while respecting individual rights and values.

Edge computing, which involves processing data closer to its source rather than relying solely on centralized cloud servers, is gaining prominence. In applications like IoT (Internet of Things) and autonomous systems, edge computing enables real-time data analysis and decision-making. The future of data science will be characterized by the ability to process and analyze vast volumes of data at the edge, resulting in faster response times and reduced latency.

The advent of quantum computing holds the promise of solving complex problems exponentially faster than classical computers. In data science, quantum algorithms can revolutionize optimization, cryptography, and simulations. Although commercial quantum computers are still in their infancy, they have the potential to transform data science by dramatically speeding up calculations and analyses.

Data visualization will continue to evolve, offering more sophisticated and interactive ways to explore and present data. Advanced visualization techniques, coupled with interpretability tools, will help data scientists and decision-makers understand complex models and results. This trend will enhance the ability to extract actionable insights from data and communicate them effectively to a wider audience.

The future of data science will see AI systems becoming increasingly personalized and context-aware. AI algorithms will be better equipped to understand individual preferences and adapt recommendations and interactions accordingly. This trend will impact fields like e-commerce, healthcare, and content recommendation, providing users with more tailored and relevant experiences.

The healthcare industry will be a focal point for data science advancements. Predictive analytics, AI-driven diagnostics, and personalized treatment plans will become more prevalent, improving patient care and outcomes. Wearable devices and remote patient monitoring will generate vast amounts of healthcare data, creating new opportunities for data-driven insights and interventions.

Data science will be crucial in addressing global challenges like climate change and sustainability. Advanced analytics and modeling will help predict environmental trends, optimize resource allocation, and inform policy decisions. The integration of data science into sustainability efforts will lead to more effective and data-driven solutions.

In the future, data science will increasingly converge with domain expertise in various fields. Data scientists will work closely with professionals in healthcare, finance, agriculture, and other domains to develop specialized solutions and insights. This collaboration will lead to more contextually relevant and impactful data science applications.

The future of data science will also see a growing emphasis on using data for social good. Data-driven initiatives will be aimed at addressing societal challenges, such as poverty, education, and public health. Data science will contribute to evidence-based policy-making and the advancement of social justice causes.

The future of data science is one of limitless potential and significant responsibility. As technology continues to advance, ethical considerations, transparency, and accountability will become even more critical. Data scientists, organizations, and policymakers must work together to ensure that data science serves not only technological innovation but also the betterment of humanity. The future landscape of data science will be shaped by a commitment to responsible practices, an integration of cutting-edge technologies, and a steadfast dedication to solving the most pressing challenges of our time. As we navigate this evolving landscape, the promise of data science to transform industries, enhance decision-making, and drive positive societal impact remains brighter than ever.

CONCLUSION

Recap of Key Concepts

In our exploration of the multifaceted realm of data science, we have delved into a myriad of key concepts, methodologies, and principles that underpin this rapidly evolving field. As we recap these fundamental ideas, we gain a holistic understanding of data science's transformative power, its applications across diverse domains, and the ethical considerations that guide its progress. From the core principles of data science to its practical implementation, we have journeyed through a rich landscape of knowledge.

At the heart of data science lie its foundational principles. Data, as the cornerstone, is the raw material from which insights are extracted. This data can be structured, semi-structured, or unstructured, and it often requires careful cleaning and preprocessing to become valuable. We have learned about the "Five Vs" of data—Volume, Velocity, Variety, Veracity, and Value—and how they characterize the complex nature of data in the modern world.

Data science projects follow a structured lifecycle, which encompasses data collection, data cleaning and preprocessing, exploratory data analysis (EDA), modeling, evaluation, and deployment. This systematic approach ensures that data-driven insights are reliable and actionable. EDA, in particular, plays a vital role in understanding data patterns and relationships.

The most advanced predictive and prescriptive techniques in data science are machine learning and deep learning. Supervised learning algorithms enable us to make predictions based on labeled training data, while unsupervised learning explores hidden patterns in unlabeled data. Deep learning, with its neural networks, has revolutionized tasks like image recognition, natural language processing, and recommendation systems.

Data science extends its reach across various industries and domains. We have explored its applications in healthcare, finance, e-commerce, and more. Predictive analytics in healthcare aids in patient diagnosis and treatment planning, while financial institutions use data science for risk assessment and fraud detection. E-commerce thrives on recommendation engines powered by data-driven insights.

Ethics and responsibility are integral to data science. We have discussed the challenges of bias in AI models, emphasizing the need for fairness-aware algorithms. Privacy concerns loom large in an era of data abundance, making data protection regulations like GDPR and CCPA essential. Ethical data collection, usage, and transparency are critical in building trust with users and stakeholders. To

ensure data quality, privacy, and compliance, organizations establish data governance frameworks. These frameworks define policies, procedures, and roles for data management, fostering a culture of data responsibility. Data governance is a continuous process that involves assessment, policy creation, stakeholder engagement, technology implementation, training, monitoring, and refinement.

An effective project management is vital for the success of data science initiatives. Agile methodologies provide the flexibility and adaptability needed in the iterative and exploratory nature of data science projects. Clear problem definition, stakeholder engagement, prototyping, and ongoing evaluation are key components of successful project management in data science.

The future of data science is marked by exciting developments. AI and automation will streamline data analysis tasks, making data science more accessible. Quantum computing holds the promise of addressing complex problems exponentially faster. Edge computing and real-time analytics will enable faster decision- making, while ethical considerations will become increasingly central.

As we recap these key concepts, it is important to recognize that the field of data science is continually evolving. Staying current with emerging technologies, ethical guidelines, and best practices is essential. Data science's potential for positive impact across various sectors is immense, and the responsible application of its principles will shape a future where data-driven insights drive progress and innovation.

The Ongoing Importance of Data Science

In the digital age, data is the lifeblood of organizations and societies alike. It flows through our interconnected world, generated by sensors, devices, and human interactions, creating a wealth of information waiting to be harnessed. This is where data science, the interdisciplinary field that extracts insights and knowledge from data, comes into play. While it has already made profound impacts across industries and domains, its importance continues to grow. In this section, we delve into the ongoing significance of data science, exploring how it empowers innovation, drives decision-making, and shapes the future.

Data science has become an essential tool for informed decision-making in both the public and private sectors. By analyzing data from diverse sources, organizations can gain helpful insights into customer behavior, market trends, and operational efficiency. In healthcare, data-driven decision-making can lead to more accurate diagnoses and personalized treatment plans. In finance, it helps institutions assess risk and make investment decisions. In government, it informs policy-making and resource allocation. In essence, data science provides the evidence-based foundation upon which better decisions are made.

Innovation often springs from the ability to see patterns, connections, and possibilities that were previously hidden. Data science, with its analytical techniques and machine learning algorithms, uncovers these hidden insights. It powers recommendation systems that suggest products and content tailored to individual preferences. It drives the development of autonomous vehicles, where vast amounts of data are processed to ensure safe navigation. It underpins the discovery of new pharmaceuticals by analyzing complex biological data. In essence, data science fuels innovation by transforming data into actionable knowledge.

One of the most visible impacts of data science is personalization. Whether you're shopping online, streaming content, or using social media, data-driven algorithms are at work to customize your experience. They analyze your past behavior, preferences, and interactions to provide recommendations and content that resonate with you. This level of personalization enhances user engagement, satisfaction, and loyalty. It demonstrates how data science can create value by tailoring experiences to individual needs and desires.

Predictive analytics, a core component of data science, has revolutionized efficiency across various sectors. Businesses employ predictive models to forecast demand, optimize supply chains, and minimize downtime. Healthcare institutions use predictive analytics to anticipate patient admission rates and allocate resources accordingly. City planners utilize it to predict traffic congestion and optimize transportation systems. In each case, predictive analytics enhances efficiency by anticipating future events and optimizing resource allocation.

Data science is transforming the healthcare landscape by enabling personalized medicine, disease prediction, and drug discovery. Genomic data analysis allows healthcare providers to tailor treatment plans to an individual's genetic makeup, improving outcomes and minimizing side effects. Predictive models can detect patients at risk of specific diseases, enabling early intervention. Data-driven drug discovery accelerates the development of new therapies. As healthcare data continues to grow, data science will be increasingly vital in improving patient care and outcomes.

Data science has become an integral part of scientific research across disciplines. Astronomers analyze vast datasets to discover exoplanets and map the universe. Climate scientists use data-driven models to predict climate trends and assess the impact of environmental changes. Social scientists employ data science to study human behavior, analyze survey responses, and identify societal patterns. The ability to process and analyze large datasets has opened new frontiers in research and expanded our understanding of the world.

As the influence of data science grows, so does the need for ethical considerations and responsible AI. Bias in algorithms and data, privacy concerns, and unintended consequences are important issues to address. Data scientists and organizations are increasingly embracing ethical frameworks and guidelines to ensure that data-driven decisions and AI applications align with societal values and respect individual rights.

The ongoing importance of data science is underscored by the road ahead. Emerging technologies like quantum computing hold the promise of solving complex problems exponentially faster. AI and automation will streamline data analysis tasks, making data science more accessible.

Edge computing and real-time analytics will enable faster decision-making, while decentralized data governance models may emerge to address data sovereignty and privacy concerns.

In conclusion, data science's ongoing importance is indisputable. It empowers organizations to make informed decisions, drives innovation across industries, and enhances user experiences. It plays a pivotal role in transforming healthcare, advancing research, and addressing societal challenges. Yet, with this importance comes the responsibility to use data science ethically and responsibly. As data continues to proliferate and technology advances, data science's role in shaping the future remains central, offering boundless opportunities for progress and innovation in an increasingly data-driven world.

Encouragement for Further Learning and Exploration

As we conclude our journey through the vast landscape of data science, it is important to acknowledge that our exploration is but a small step into the boundless realm of knowledge. The field of data science, characterized by its ever-evolving nature, continually presents new challenges, opportunities, and avenues for discovery. In this section, we offer words of encouragement for further learning and exploration, emphasizing the value of lifelong curiosity, the dynamic nature of technology, and the ethical responsibilities that come with wielding data-driven insights.

In the world of data science, learning is not a destination but a journey. The knowledge you have gained is a foundation upon which to build, and the field itself is in perpetual motion. New algorithms, tools, and techniques emerge regularly, and staying up-to-date is essential. Whether through online courses, books, academic programs, or peer-to-peer collaboration, the thirst for knowledge should remain unquenchable.

The tools at your disposal as a data scientist are constantly evolving. From machine learning frameworks to data visualization libraries, the technology stack evolves to make your work more efficient and powerful. Embrace this evolution, experiment with new tools, and adapt your skills to remain at the cutting edge of data science.

With great power comes great responsibility. As you delve deeper into data science, remember the ethical considerations that underpin the field. Bias mitigation, privacy protection, and responsible AI are not mere buzzwords but essential principles that should guide your work. Strive to use data science for the betterment of society, respecting the rights and dignity of individuals.

Data science thrives in collaboration with other fields. Embrace interdisciplinary learning and collaboration with experts from diverse domains. The fusion of data science with healthcare, finance, environmental science, and more holds the potential for groundbreaking discoveries and innovative solutions to complex problems.

Data science involves more than simply math computations; it's about solving real-world problems. Approach each challenge with a problem-solving mindset, asking the right questions, and leveraging data to find answers. The ability to translate data-driven insights into actionable solutions is a hallmark of a successful data scientist.

Seek mentorship and actively participate in the data science community. Mentorship provides guidance, insights, and a support system to navigate the intricacies of the field. Engaging with the community through forums, conferences, and meetups fosters networking and collaborative learning.

The only constant in data science is change. Be prepared to adapt to new data sources, emerging technologies, and evolving best practices. Adaptability is a valuable trait that allows you to thrive in an ever-changing landscape.

Challenges are opportunities for growth. When faced with a daunting problem or a complex dataset, see it as a chance to learn and innovate. The most rewarding discoveries often arise from tackling the most formidable challenges.

As you learn and grow in your data science journey, don't forget to give back. Share your knowledge and experiences with others. Mentoring, teaching, or contributing to open-source projects can be immensely fulfilling and can help the data science community flourish.

Curiosity is the driving force behind all great discoveries. Never lose your sense of wonder and curiosity about the world and the data within it. Explore new questions, seek novel perspectives, and approach data science with an inquisitive spirit.

In conclusion, data science is a journey of perpetual learning and exploration. The knowledge you've acquired is a stepping stone, and the path ahead is illuminated by the infinite possibilities of data-driven discovery. Embrace the evolving nature of technology, uphold ethical principles, collaborate across disciplines, and remain adaptable in the face of change. Most importantly, nurture your curiosity, for it is the key to unlocking the endless horizons of knowledge that data science offers. As you continue your voyage, may you find inspiration in the mysteries of data and the transformative potential it holds for our world.

Thank you for buying and reading/ listening to our book. If you found this book useful/ helpful please take a few minutes and leave a review on the platform where you purchased our book. Your feedback matters greatly to us.